The Whisper *of* Purpose

The Whisper of Purpose

Finding Meaning and Direction in a Noisy World

FELICIA BESSMAN

The Whisper of Purpose © Copyright 2025 Felicia Bessman

All rights reserved. No part of this publication may be reproduced, distributed or transmitted in any form or by any means, including photocopying, recording, or other electronic or mechanical methods, without the prior written permission of the publisher, except in the case of brief quotations embodied in critical reviews and certain other noncommercial uses permitted by copyright law.

Although the author and publisher have made every effort to ensure that the information in this book was correct at press time, the author and publisher do not assume and hereby disclaim any liability to any party for any loss, damage, or disruption caused by errors or omissions, whether such errors or omissions result from negligence, accident, or any other cause.

Adherence to all applicable laws and regulations, including international, federal, state and local governing professional licensing, business practices, advertising, and all other aspects of doing business in the US, Canada or any other jurisdiction is the sole responsibility of the reader and consumer.

Neither the author nor the publisher assumes any responsibility or liability whatsoever on behalf of the consumer or reader of this material. Any perceived slight of any individual or organization is purely unintentional.

The resources in this book are provided for informational purposes only and should not be used to replace the specialized training and professional judgment of a health care or mental health care professional.

Neither the author nor the publisher can be held responsible for the use of the information provided within this book. Please always consult a trained professional before making any decision regarding treatment of yourself or others.

For more information, email frankokeefe25@gmail.com

ISBN: 979-8-89694-947-3 - Ebook
ISBN: 979-8-89694-948-0 - Paperback
ISBN: 979-8-89694-949-7 - Hardcover

Dedication

To my beloved mom (now deceased), who inspired me to walk in purpose.

To my husband, Bishop Bessman, for his loving support. To my dearest children, Daphane and Theo Jr., who gave me purpose. To my beloved granddaughter, Chassidy, who is my inspiration and cheerleader.

To my New Grace Church family, who continuously bestows love and grace upon me, and to my prayer-line leaders for their relentless prayers.

To my church youth and their leader, Minister Cece Jones, for inspiring me and praying diligently for our church leadership during difficult seasons.

To my friends, colleagues (especially Rita Gallaway, Stelna Chennat, and Dr. Christian Garrett), mentors, and counselors—your wisdom, patience, and thoughtful conversations helped shape the ideas that echo through these pages. You reminded me that purpose is not always loud, but it is always present.

And to everyone who cheered me on, checked in, or just "nodded politely"—this book is for you.

And to the voice in my head that whispered, "You can do this"—thank you for nudging loudly and repeatedly.

Contents

Acknowledgments		9
Foreword		13
Foreword 2		15
Preface		17
How to Use This Book		19
Introduction		21
1	When Silence Speaks The Loudest	23
2	The Nudge You Can't Ignore	39
3	Discerning The Voice Within	53
4	Called But Not Yet Sent	63
5	Purpose In Pieces	75
6	Permission To Obey	89
7	The Assignment That Found You	101
8	When Doors Close Softly	115
9	Faithfulness In The Fog	127
10	Living Loudly From A Whisper	141
Closing		
Let the Whisper Echo		157
Additional Resources		159
About the Author		163

Acknowledgments

Writing *The Whisper of Purpose* has been a journey of reflection, discovery, and quiet determination. This book would not have come to life without the unwavering support, inspiration, and encouragement of many remarkable souls.

To my daughter, Daphane—my living inspiration. You've got a spirit that refuses to dim and a tenacity that sparked momentum for this very book. Your love and your unwavering belief in me gave me the courage to lean in, to hear the quiet voice within, and to follow it—boldly and without fear. Thank you for standing beside me, for helping to type this manuscript, and for lighting the path with your spirit.

I extend my deepest gratitude **to my spiritual daughter, Deacon Lamne Johnson**, whose quiet and gentle nudges have been a steady light in my spiritual journey. As my spiritual daughter and an exceptional Bible teacher, Lamne's wisdom and grace have enriched my walk and reminded me of the beauty found in sacred stillness.

To my prayer warrior daughters, Yamah Phillips and Sonnie Mulbah, whose relentless devotion to all-night intercession became a sacred lifeline during some of my hardest seasons. Your faithfulness was not just felt; it carried me.

To Deacon Williette Morris, my prayer-line leader and a pastor's wife, whose love is both steady and sacred. Your consistent check-ins have been more than kindness—they've been a soul-lifter, a gentle stirring toward purpose.

To my cherished Ghanaian spiritual daughter, Vivien Gyimah—your sweet spirit has lifted mine like the rhythm of Adowa drums: joyful, steady, deeply rooted. During seasons of weariness, your check-ins, warm encouragement, and nourishing meals were seasoned with love. You've walked with me as only a daughter of grace can.

To the most cherished elder in my life, Mama Bertha Vawar, once my fourth-grade teacher, now a beloved member of my church family. Your words have always tasted of honey: sweet, healing, and steadfast. You call me just to check on my heart, to speak peace into my storms, and to remind me—again and again—that it will be okay.

To **Lorina Stemn and Euphemia Moore**, my church women's leaders and spiritual daughters, whose quiet fortitude, consistency, and radiant grace speak volumes where words fall short. In every season, their steadfast devotion and presence have woven hope into the lives of many sisters.

To Elaina Hall (Laini), another beloved spiritual daughter whose life blossoms with service and generosity. As our church hospitality leader, she creates a sacred space where strangers become family. Her quiet strength reminds us that hospitality is holy work.

To my best friend forever (BFF), Fay Cooper—thank you for embodying enduring love and steadfast sisterhood.

Acknowledgments

Your commitment to our bond and the countless words of encouragement you've shared have echoed through the seasons of my life, reminding me that true friendship is both a gift and a shelter.

And **to Pastor Wendy Harmon**, whose heart reflects the beauty of pastoral care. Your willingness to pause, answer my calls, uplift my spirit, and pray with me has brought warmth and light when I needed it most. You exemplify grace in action and the sacred ministry of being present.

Each of these **remarkable women** has not only blessed my life with their compassion and faithfulness but has also reflected God's love in tangible, unforgettable ways. I am eternally grateful for the divine tapestry of friendship and spiritual kinship we share.

To the readers, thank you for opening your hearts to my story. May it whisper to you in the moments you need it most, and may it guide you gently toward truth.

I extend quiet thanks for the guided support received behind the scenes.

And finally, to the quiet moments, the stillness, and the whispers that sparked this book, thank you for reminding me that purpose often speaks in silence.

With deep gratitude,

Felicia **(Fefe)**

Foreword

In a world where the cacophony of daily life often drowns out the whispers of our inner calling, *The Whisper of Purpose* emerges as a beacon of hope and guidance. Dr. Felicia Bessman, affectionately known as Ma Fefe, has crafted a memoir that is not just a book but a spiritual companion for those navigating the often-murky waters of divine direction.

Dr. Bessman's unique blend of clinical clarity and spiritual mentorship offers readers a roadmap to discern God's quiet invitations. Her reflections on obedience in obscurity, the courage to act, and the divine permission to move forward with only a fragment of the vision are both profound and practical. Each chapter is a treasure trove of anchored Scriptures, reflections, spiritual formation tools, and actionable steps that guide readers toward a deeper understanding of their purpose.

As a Clinical Assistant Professor of Nursing, an executive pastor, and a mentor to emerging spiritual leaders, Dr. Bessman's teachings span academic, spiritual, and relational circles. *The Whisper of Purpose* is more than a memoir; it is an invitation to recognize and respond to the sacred moments in our lives. It is a call to listen for the divine whisper and to find purpose in the everyday.

This book is for anyone who has ever felt overlooked, underprepared, or spiritually in-between. It speaks to those who have questioned their call amidst a busy calendar and a hungry soul. This book is a must-read for anyone seeking to deepen their spiritual journey and embrace their God-given purpose.

Enjoy this treasure!

—Lamne Johnson-Bright
Deacon Chair, Bible Study Leader, New Grace, Arlington

Foreword 2

I have had the gift of knowing Dr. Felicia Bessman as a true sister in Christ, first by the power of Holy Spirit. Our meeting and growth in relationship have been without trying and evidence of God's love and desire for us. She is the truth she speaks. I watched Felicia navigate through the processes of this book's content long before she ever thoroughly conceived that this rich treasure would even become. She would disappear for periods of time immersing herself in the presence of God, in her secret and sacred place. I have always known what her brief absences meant.

This beautiful and honest work was not written to advance Felicia's platform, but rather to lead others into greater visual of God's will being fulfilled, in and through us even in spaces where we sometimes feel the most desolate and alone. It is life rendering. Carefully presented to us as fruit of time spent with God. A work that reveals its author's heart to do HIS will and not her own. From the desire to be more like Christ by the literal guidance of the Holy spirit not just a feeling.

The Whisper of Purpose is a quiet book just as the title indicates. It breathes slowly and encourages the reader to do the very same. Felicia does not write in a way that would indicate she has all the answers, but rather thoughtfully, honestly, and tenderly provoking consideration of answers we seek from God regarding purpose and revealing the beauty of his gentle responses and the beauty found in his whispers and gentle nudging.

Felicia's message is for those of us who believe that we have a clear God given purpose yet still travel through foggy places receiving only small pieces of the vision at a time, which in truth is most of us.

The Whisper of Purpose is for everyone. The chapters will make us feel as though we are spending the evening in cozy chairs over a cup of tea or cocoa with a long-time friend and the Lord Himself. We find Him here and are led by Him.

Felicia, thank you for not waiting until everything was perfect to share this with us. Thank you for your transparency and for trusting God enough to let Him guide your pen and heart from the middle of your own personal circumstances where you continue to seek His voice for your very own "nexts".

Thank you for demonstrating what bravery really looks like, waiting silence. Thank you for listening and trusting in "Our Father's" whisperings to you.

I pray all those who read this sweet gift will not rush. Allow this to read you as much as you read it. Let it remind you that Jesus still leads with love, that the Holy Spirit still speaks in whispers, and that your purpose regardless of your perceived size of it – is truly holy and necessary. Wow God! Thank you, Jesus! Thank you, Holy Spirit. I am honored and humbled by the invitation to contribute in this way.

Celebrating with the deepest love, respect and pure joy for this moment in time.

—Fay Cooper
Friend, Sister, Witness, and Kindred Listener

Preface

This book was never meant to be written quickly. It was whispered into my spirit over time—through seasons of silence, surrender, and sacred discomfort. I didn't set out to write a book about purpose. I set out to obey. And in doing so, I discovered that obedience itself is often the birthplace of purpose.

The Whisper of Purpose was born from moments when I questioned my calling, questioned my worth, delayed my yes, and wrestled with the tension between divine nudges and human hesitation. I've learned that purpose rarely arrives with clarity—it often comes wrapped in whispers and messes. Whispers that challenge, convict, and call us deeper.

This book is my journey about the nudges I felt but hesitated to move for. I heard God speak but waited for confirmation. I was afraid that obedience might cost too much. So I wrote this book, not just for me, but for anyone who is hearing the whisper and is unsure about the next steps.

Each chapter is an invitation—not just to reflect, but to respond. To listen for the whisper, to surrender the fear, and to step into the sacred unknown with faith. My prayer is that these pages will stir something in you that cannot be ignored. That you'll hear the whisper again—and this time, you'll say yes.

With grace and expectancy,

Felicia Bessman (Fefe)

How to Use This Book

A gentle guide for the journey ahead.

Inhale the whisper, exhale the weight.

This is not a race. It's a rhythm.

You're holding space, not just a book. It's a space to pause, reflect, breathe, and listen. Each chapter in The Whisper of Purpose *is designed as a sacred conversation—between you, the Spirit, and your unfolding sense of purpose.*

1. Go Slow

This isn't meant to be devoured in one sitting. Let each chapter breathe. Read one per day, one per week, or as the Spirit leads. Make space for the whisper to become clear.

2. Reflect Deeply

After every chapter, you'll find prompts. Use these tools to engage with what's rising in you—grief, clarity, conviction, joy. All are welcome here.

3. Listen with Openness

Expect God to speak—not always with answers, but with alignment. Keep a pen nearby, a soft heart, and a quiet space. You may hear something that shifts everything.

4. Return Often

This book is a companion for more than one season. Come back when you're tired, confused, or ready to obey again. Let it echo differently with each return.

God still speaks. And the whisper still leads.

Introduction

There is a whisper that echoes beyond the noise of everyday life—a sacred stirring that refuses to be silenced. It's subtle, yet persistent. Gentle, yet disruptive. It's *The Whisper of Purpose*. This book is for the soul that senses there's more. For the one who's felt the nudge but hesitated. For the believer who's heard God's call but wrestled with timing, fear, or the weight of obedience.

The Whisper of Purpose is not a manual; it's a mirror. A spiritual companion that reflects the tension between divine invitation and human hesitation. Each chapter is a doorway into deeper reflection, biblical insight, and spiritual activation. You'll walk alongside figures like Mary, Abraham, Elijah, and Esther—people who heard the whisper and chose to respond, even when the cost was great. You'll be invited to name your own delays, confront your fears, and declare permission to move forward.

This is a journey of surrender. Of listening more closely. Trusting that the whisper you've heard is not your imagination—it's your invitation.

You don't need to shout to be called. Sometimes, purpose speaks in a whisper. And it's time to listen.

1

When Silence Speaks The Loudest

When silence speaks the loudest, it honors the weight of spiritual quietness and divine restraint.

This chapter invites you to

- reflect on moments when silence carried more truth than words.
- explore biblical examples like Jesus before Pilate, Hannah in prayer, and Job in suffering.
- practice listening for divine messages in quiet seasons.
- surrender the need to fill silence with noise or justification.
- declare trust in God's voice, even when it's still.

In the sacred hush of Psalm 46:10, we are invited into a divine stillness: "Be still, and know that I am God! I will be honored by every nation. I will be honored throughout the world" (Psalm 46:10, NLT). This verse is not merely a call to pause; it is a summons to be present, to relinquish control, and to encounter the holy in the quiet. In a world that prizes productivity and noise, stillness becomes a radical act of trust. It is in the silence that we cease striving and begin receiving—not necessarily answers, but awareness. The knowing that follows stillness is not intellectual; it is spiritual, intimate, and transformative.

This is what happened to me some years ago, when I was trying to decide whether to go to grad school, which was my initial plan. As a nurse, I wanted to advance my career in the area of nurse anesthesia. After meeting all the criteria to enroll in this program, I changed my mind after I heard the whisper that said, "Be still for now." That's when I abandoned the idea of going to grad school for nurse anesthesia. Even with the busyness of raising small children, working alongside my husband in ministry, and working full-time, I was able to hear the whisper.

The constant buzz of modern life and distraction drown out divine direction. While I heard the whisper to abandon grad school for nursing, I did not hear the whispers for the next steps. In an age where notifications flood our senses and the hurry of life shouts louder than our thoughts, the quiet voice of God often goes unheard—not because He isn't speaking, but because we've become unaccustomed to listening. I was not listening.

> *The constant buzz of modern life and distraction drown out divine direction.*

The world is addicted to noise: podcasts and playlists for every moment, commentaries for every decision, endless scrolling designed to keep our souls suspended in a state of distraction. Yet amid the chaos, Scripture reminds us that the Almighty rarely shouts; He whispers. You might expect purpose to arrive with volume: a sign, a crowd, or a sudden certainty. But sometimes, it comes in silence.

No spotlight. No booming voice. Just holy stillness, pressing into your anxious thoughts like soft rain on dry ground, like it did for me. A silence that doesn't abandon you but *invites* you to be still long enough to hear what activity drowns out. I was asking God to speak louder. But what if He was waiting for me to become quieter?

So years later, after my husband and I felt called to start a church ministry in another city away from where we had served for seven years, I could finally hear the silence of divine whisper.

A whisper is so intimate, it assumes proximity. God's whisper isn't always audible—it's a prompting, a nudge, a verse that repeats in our hearts. It may come as a sudden clarity during prayer, a conviction when reading His Word, or an unusual peace in the middle of a storm.

> *A whisper is so intimate, it assumes proximity.*

And so, with God's constant promptings, timely Scriptures, and spiritual mentors, my husband and I decided to obey the whisper and started a church. We had thirteen members, all of whom were people in our couples' fellowship group and their family members. These whispers were soft but pressing. The Divine does not speak softly to strangers, only to beloved children who've chosen intimacy over performance. To recognize His whisper is to acknowledge that He desires communion, not spectacle. Whispers aren't random—they're relational cues. God doesn't need to yell to be authoritative. He whispers to draw us near, and His whispers drew me near.

The Power of Silence

We live in a world that celebrates noise. From the moment we wake up, we are bombarded with notifications, news, conversations, and content. Silence has become uncomfortable, even suspicious. Yet, in the stillness—when the world quiets down—something sacred happens. It is in these moments that the divine often chooses to speak. But how do we hear God in a world that never stops talking?

Noise isn't just sound; it's distraction. It's the mental clutter, the emotional static, the spiritual fog that keeps us from tuning in to the frequency of heaven. We fill our lives with busyness, often mistaking motion for meaning (guilty as charged). The world's volume isn't just loud; it's chronic. We've mistaken stimulation for significance. Busyness for productivity. Popularity for purpose.

Noise can manifest in many ways:

- **Social noise:** endless opinions, curated personas, and the pressure to respond
- **Emotional noise:** internal chatter fueled by anxiety, comparison, and unmet expectations
- **Spiritual noise:** the compulsion to "do" in ministry rather than "be" with the One who calls you
- **Cultural addiction to noise:** social media, entertainment, constant productivity

A common undercurrent of noise is **a fear of silence**. We avoid stillness, and this reveals something about us, such as fear of being misunderstood by others or of appearing weak. While this fear seems difficult to conquer, resilience in these moments will help you overcome such fear and push forward toward your goal.

This noise isn't just environmental; it's formational. It shapes our ability to discern, distorts our spiritual compass, and dulls our sensitivity to divine direction.

Silence as Sanctuary

In Scripture, silence is never empty—in fact, it's often the loudest language of faith. Jesus stood before Pilate, bruised and accused, yet chose not to defend Himself. His silence fulfilled prophecy (Isaiah 53:7) and thundered with surrender to the Father's will, revealing that truth doesn't always need a rebuttal to be victorious. Hannah, in the temple, prayed without words; her lips moved, but no sound came (1 Samuel 1:13). Misunderstood by Eli, her silent plea carried the weight of years of longing, and God heard what no one else could. Job, stripped of everything, sat in ashes while heaven seemed quiet. His silence wasn't weakness—it was the sacred space where questions met trust, and where God would eventually speak from the whirlwind (Job 38). In each story, silence became a sanctuary, a place where faith was refined, purpose was revealed, and heaven leaned in close.

God called young Samuel repeatedly at night, and Samuel learned to recognize and respond: *"Speak, your servant is listening"* (1 Sam. 3:10, NLT). Jesus withdrew to solitary places to pray (Matt. 14:13, Luke 6:12). The Spirit

> *Silence is not the absence of God; it's often the space where He is most present.*

nudged Philip to approach the Ethiopian eunuch's chariot, leading to the eunuch's baptism (Acts 8:34–38). Silence is not the absence of God; it's often the space where He is most present.

Elijah, weary and disillusioned, experienced this in 1 Kings 19. Expecting God to show up in wind, earthquake, or fire, he discovered instead a "still small voice" (1 Kings 19:12, NKJV). That voice wasn't diminished by its softness; it was amplified by the stillness required to hear it.

Whispers imply relationships. While God sometimes speaks to unbelievers for the purpose of transforming them (e.g., Paul's conversion on the road to Damascus, Acts 9:3–6), He whispers to believers to align them with purpose. To recognize His whisper is to acknowledge that He desires communion, not spectacle.

Recognizing Divine Whispers

At its core, a **divine whisper** is a subtle, Spirit-borne communication from God—distinct not in its volume but in its intimacy, timing, and transformative power. Unlike prophetic visions or thunderous declarations, divine whispers often arrive quietly, requiring spiritual sensitivity to detect and courage to obey. Here's what makes whispers unique:

- **Subtle but persistent**: I did not hear a loud voice, but the same message kept surfacing—through Scripture, prayer, conversations, and even nature.
- **Deeply personal**: The whispers were tailored to my life, my journey, and my calling. They rarely felt generic; they pierced right where I was.

- **Aligned with Scripture**: They never contradict God's Word; rather, they often illuminate it. I found the whispers were more clarifying than confusing.
- **Timing-sensitive**: They often came when I was quiet, receptive, and still, such as in early morning meditations, late-night reflections, and mid-ministry moments of vulnerability.
- **Easy to dismiss**: Because they don't demand attention, they require discernment. The enemy shouts; God whispers and invites. He never coerces.

How to Recognize a Whisper from Our Own Personal Thoughts

So how can you separate a divine whisper from wordly noise? Let's break down the difference:

Feature	Divine Whisper	Worldly Noise
Tone	Gentle, persistent	Loud, urgent
Effect	Peace, clarity	Anxiety, confusion
Source	Scripture-based, Spirit-led	External media, social opinion
Invitation	Requires stillness and surrender	Demands reaction and rush

You can sense a whisper by its fruit. Does it lead to deeper trust, obedience, and peace? Or does it escalate panic and push performance? If we want to hear God, we must make space for Him. This means intentional silence, solitude, and surrender. I had to get away for a personal silence retreat in order to hear the whispers clearly during certain seasons of my life. While this was less about escaping the world and more about creating sacred rhythms within it, I needed the space to hear.

Hearing in the Midst of Ministry Work

Even spiritual work can be noisy. I know this well, from church rooms to classrooms to clinics. A whisper doesn't compete with your schedule; it waits for your surrender. This is what happened to me. I was working as a nurse, in seminary for a dual master's in counseling and Christian education, and working alongside my husband in bivocational ministry. Talk about busy; I was the queen!

For us, bivocational meant working a full-time secular job and doing full-time ministry work. This was not because we wanted double the money, but because the church could not afford to cover our salaries and insurance. Amid all this busyness, God kept whispering and waiting for my surrender. To get to surrender, I began to use Jesus' model of retreating frequently and regularly. Jesus did this not because He lacked strength, but because He desired intimacy. I did it because I both lacked strength and desired intimacy. I know that Jesus' private prayers fueled His public ministry, and I wanted that too.

What I learned was that if I wanted to hear the whisper amid responsibilities, I had to do the following:

- **Pause in-between productivity.** The Spirit speaks in transitions.
- **Return to the altar, not just the pulpit.** The altar is where you bring your worship, and the pulpit is where you proclaim the message God gives you.

- **Let silence speak louder than metrics.** Sometimes, the most spiritually fruitful decision is to step away from the applause and sit quietly with God.
- **Pray when everything is fine.** Pray when you're doing well physically, emotionally, and/or spiritually. Because I had so much to do, I couldn't afford not to pray.
- **Pray when you're struggling.** Continue to pray when the situation seems dim.
- **Pray in the morning, at noontime, and at night.** Let your prayer work around the clock. David, the great king of Israel, used this schedule and testified to many breakthroughs. Let your prayers be a special time that you look forward to sharing with your heavenly Father.
- **Pray in between scheduled prayers.** Praying in between those scheduled times just adds more commitment to your prayer life and helps you hear the whispers more.
- **Seek wisdom from the word of God.** "If any of you lacks wisdom, you should ask God, who gives generously to all without finding fault, and it will be given to you" (James 1:5, NIV).
- **Find rest and take it.** Tiredness is not a sin. If God rested, you can too. You hear clearly when you are rested.
- **Don't feel guilty about rest**. Rest doesn't mean laziness, even if people perceive it that way.
- **Use your heart before your body.** By using our heart first, we surrender totally to God and listen for His whisper.

If this list seems overwhelming, pick one or two actions and start there. The goal is not to add to your list of to-dos, but to meet with God where you are today.

Cultivating a Whisper-Sensitive Life

If you want to hear whispers, you must create space. Like preparing a sanctuary, our hearts must be conditioned to receive.

Here are a few habits that restore sensitivity to God's voice and that helped me to hear the whispers more:

1. Practice Sacred Pauses

Before rushing into the next task, breathe. Pause between conversations. Before answering, pray inwardly. Sacred pauses train our spirit to wait, and waiting makes room for whispers.

2. Engage in Deep Listening

Whispers aren't received through multitasking. Give God the gift of your full attention. When you pray, listen more than you speak. When you study Scripture, don't ask, "What does this mean?" Instead, ask, "What are You saying to me right now?"

3. Create Noise-Free Zones

Designate spaces and times in your day where silence reigns. Let your morning coffee be consumed in worship, not headlines. Let your walks echo Scripture, not Spotify or Facebook algorithms.

4. Attend the Spirit's Nudge

God often speaks in ways that feel subtle and inconvenient, yet they are unmistakably purposeful. It might be a sudden wave of compassion for someone who's hurting, a strong urge to pray even when you're weary, or a phrase or Scripture that lingers in your mind long after you've heard it. These moments are not random. They are gentle invitations, divine whispers that beckon your attention. Rather than dismiss them as fleeting thoughts, pause and ask, "Lord, are You whispering here?" With that question, you open the door to discernment and obedience.

Practical Disciplines

Disciplines create space for divine encounter. Silence and solitude offer a sacred pause, allowing the noise of the world to settle so the whisper of God can rise. Journaling and reflection help us trace the movement of the Spirit in our lives, giving language to what we're learning and feeling. Digital detox and Sabbath rest restore our attention and remind us that our worth is not tied to productivity. Sacred spaces—whether a quiet corner, a candlelit room, or a walk in nature—become environments that invite God's presence and foster intimacy. And listening itself becomes worship when we honor God by giving Him our full attention, not just with our ears but with our hearts. These disciplines are not tasks to complete; they are rhythms that shape us into people who are present, attentive, and responsive to the Spirit.

When Silence Feels Empty

Sometimes, silence doesn't feel sacred; it feels like absence. We pray and hear nothing. We wait and feel forgotten. The heavens seem still, and our hearts wonder if we've been overlooked. But scripture reminds us that even in the silence, God is working. His silence is not His absence. Job sat in ashes, David cried out in the wilderness, and Jesus hung on the cross, asking why God had forsaken Him. In each of those moments, God was present, even when He felt distant.

Silence teaches us lessons that noise cannot. It stretches our trust, deepens our patience, and refines our faith. In the quiet, we learn to anchor ourselves not in answers, but in presence. We begin to recognize that faith is not always about hearing but about holding on. When God seems silent, we are invited to remain rooted, to stay in the story, to believe that something is forming beneath the surface.

It is in the silence that the eventual whisper becomes most clear. So to the listener who feels forgotten, you are not missing it. God is speaking. His voice may be quiet, but it is present. His timing may feel slow, but it is intentional. You are not abandoned; you are being formed. Stay in the silence. Stay in the story. The whisper is coming.

Testimonies of Silence

Real stories bring this truth to life. Whether it's a moment of clarity in prayer, a quiet conviction that changed a life, or a decision made in stillness that altered destiny, God's whispers are powerful. There came a season when silence became my sanctuary. I once felt compelled to answer every criticism, to defend every careless word. But the more I spoke, the more entangled things became.

So, I made a decision: *If God wasn't speaking, neither would I.* And in that sacred hush, I found clarity. Psalm 46:10 whispered, "Be still and know that I am God," and Isaiah 30:15 echoed, "In quietness and trust is your strength" (NIV). These words were no longer distant promises—they became my lived experience. His voice grew louder in the quiet. What once felt like restraint became the very gateway to peace, wisdom, and divine direction.

The Courage to Obey a Whisper

Whispers are easy to ignore. They don't come with fanfare. But they carry divine instructions. Recognizing the whisper is only half the journey—obeying it is where transformation begins.

God may whisper a number of things to you:

- "Reach out to her."
- "Say no to that opportunity."
- "Forgive him."
- "Wait."

Whispers lead us into deeper alignment, but they require discernment and courage. They rarely make sense from a worldly perspective, but they always carry eternal significance.

> *Whispers lead us into deeper alignment, but they require discernment and courage.*

From Noise to Narrative

As of writing *The Whisper of Purpose*, I recognize that this tension between divine subtlety and worldly clamor is central. Please know that clarity doesn't always roar—it sometimes whispers through the cracks of an overloaded life, like mine.

By learning to listen, I am inviting you to rewrite your spiritual rhythm: from chaos to cadence, from clamor to communion.

Practice: Journaling in Solitude

Journaling in solitude became a practice of entering solitude with intention as I nightly reflected on my day or week. With pen in hand, I would trace the contours of my inner landscape, naming what I felt, what I feared, what I hoped. The act of writing slows us down, anchoring our thoughts in the present moment. It is not about crafting perfect prose, but about listening deeply—to God, to our own hearts, to the truths that rise in the quiet. Journaling becomes a mirror, reflecting not just our circumstances but the divine presence within them.

So we ask, What truths emerge in the quiet? Often, they are truths we've long buried beneath busyness—truths of belovedness, of calling, of healing. In the stillness, we remember who we are and whose we are. We see with clarity what matters most—and, perhaps most profoundly, we discover that God is not waiting for us to perform, but to be. To be still. To be known. To be held in the sanctuary of silence.

Reflection and Application

Scripture Focus: *"He was oppressed, yet when he was afflicted, He opened not His mouth..."* (Isaiah 53:7, ASV)

Devotional Thought: Sometimes, heaven's loudest yes comes wrapped in silence. In seasons of delay, unanswered prayer, or restrained response, God is not absent—He is cultivating trust, deepening our obedience, and inviting us into His mystery. Jesus, in His silence before His accusers, modeled surrendered strength. The absence of defense became a declaration of purpose. His quietness was thunderous with resolve.

Questions for Reflection:

- When was the last time you truly sat in silence?
- What distractions most often keep you from hearing God?
- Have you ever experienced a "whisper" moment that changed your direction?
- What has God's silence taught you about His character?
- When have you felt invited into deeper trust through unanswered prayers?
- Where might God be forming holiness in the quiet spaces of your life?

Action Steps:

- Schedule ten minutes of silence daily this week. Journal what you sense, feel, or hear in that time.
- Identify one area of your life where you need to turn down the noise.

- Write a one-sentence declaration of trust and post it somewhere visible. Let it be your silent agreement with heaven's slow and sacred work.

Prayer:

"Lord, help me to quiet the noise around me so I can hear Your whisper. Teach me to value stillness and to recognize Your voice in the silence. Teach me to lean into Your quiet. When You do not speak, let me listen for Your presence. Make my heart still enough to hear the whisper of purpose embedded in silence. Strengthen me with the courage to wait and the faith to obey. Amen."

2

The Nudge You Can't Ignore

The nudge you can't ignore carries the pulse of divine urgency and sacred interruption.

This chapter invites you to

- reflect on subtle spiritual promptings you've brushed aside.
- explore biblical examples like Samuel's call, Esther's courage, and Paul's vision.
- practice identifying the difference between impulse and divine nudge.
- surrender resistance to inconvenient obedience.
- declare readiness to respond to God's gentle push.

In Acts 9:5, we encounter Saul on the road to Damascus, confronted by a voice that pierces through his mission: "It is hard for you to kick against the goads" (NKJV). A goad is a pointed stick used to guide livestock, and here it becomes a metaphor for divine direction: gentle yet firm, persistent yet patient. Saul's resistance is not met with wrath but with revelation. This moment marks the beginning of surrender, where the nudge of God becomes undeniable. It reminds us that divine guidance often comes not as a shout, but as a repeated tap on the shoulder—an invitation we've ignored, a truth we've avoided, a calling we've delayed.

The nudge you can't ignore often comes quietly, but it carries the weight of destiny. Samuel heard it in the stillness of night: a voice he didn't yet recognize, calling him by name (1 Samuel 3). That divine nudge awakened a prophet. Esther felt it in the tension of crisis, when Mordecai's words pierced her hesitation: "Who knows whether you have come to the kingdom for such a time as this?" (Esther 4:14, NKJV). Her courage to respond saved a nation. Paul received it in a vision: a man from Macedonia pleading for help (Acts 16:9). That nudge redirected the Gospel into Europe and changed history. Each of them could have dismissed the moment, but instead they leaned in. The nudge wasn't loud, but it was unmistakable. It was God's whisper wrapped in urgency, inviting them to step into purpose that would echo far beyond their own lives.

Immediately after college, I set out to go to medical school. I took the MCAT and got accepted into medical school, but at the end of my orientation, I was faced with the cruel fact that as a foreign student, I did not qualify for financial aid, meaning I would have to cover any expenses that my academic scholarship did not cover. With this painful truth, I packed my bags and left Illinois. All our plans changed. By "our plans," I mean mine and my then-boyfriend's (now my husband). We had planned to attend grad school together in the same city. He had to abandon his plan when mine fell through—or so I thought, not knowing that God was whispering and shaping my destiny for something far greater. At the time, however, I ignored the nudge. At this juncture, I resisted divine alignment with my calling.

There are moments in life when heaven leans in. Not loudly, but insistently. Not with spectacle, but with certainty. These are the divine nudges: holy invitations clothed in ordinary moments, calling us to obey, pivot, speak, or surrender. They stir something deep, often quiet but unmistakable. And when ignored, they don't disappear—they simply wait, unwavering, for our yes. These nudges were not always convenient for me, but they were always convicting. It's that moment in prayer when your heart tightens around a name. It's the dream you can't shake, the Scripture that won't let go, the feeling that you "must act on this." Unlike divine whispers, which soothe and clarify, nudges often agitate.

Oh yes, I was agitated that my "plans" fell through. These nudges were restless. But that's the point: They remind you that God's plans rarely fit into tidy calendars or predictable schedules. The nudge is a persistent thought, a recurring burden, or a sense that something needs to change. All this time, I thought it was God who needed to hear me out, when in fact, I should have been responding to the nudges.

What the Nudge Sounds Like

If divine whispers are gentle breezes, nudges are spiritual elbow jabs. Here's what they sounded like in my spirit:

- *"There's more I've called you to."* (Not medical school, Lord?)
- *"Go back and reconcile."* (Why? They offended me; I did nothing wrong.)

- *"Apply even if you're afraid."*
- *"That person needs your compassion today."* (They never appreciate all I have already done.)
- *"You were made for this."* (For pain?)

These nudges interrupt the narrative we've built around our limitations. They contradict fear, comfort, and even logic. God's nudge for me to go to nursing school instead was not logical. My high school yearbook said that I was most likely to become a doctor, which was always my goal; I love the sciences and was always "playing doctor." But I could not kick against the goads any longer, so I finally pivoted toward nursing school. Today, without a doubt, not pursuing medical school was a divine interruption for my good.

Divine Tap on the Shoulder

The metaphor of the divine tap on the shoulder evokes a God who is both near and intentional. These taps are not interruptions; they are invitations. They ask us to pay attention, to reconsider, to turn. Like Saul, we may find that resistance itself exhausting. The goads are not punishments but prompts toward transformation.

This divine tap on the shoulder happened to me as I kept postponing going to seminary to equip myself for the work we were doing in ministry. I was counseling and teaching out of books with spiritual guidance, but I wanted to do this beyond just meeting the needs of church members. I wanted to extend this to the community and to those who were hurting. So, I thought about going to seminary to prepare for a counseling ministry, but again, I got too busy with the noise that I could not hear the whispers or feel the nudge—noise such as constant conflict resolution between church members, enmeshment in church and marital discourse, enmeshment in community activities, and everyday life.

Scriptural Echoes of the Nudge

Scripture is soaked in stories of nudged lives. The Lord didn't wait for optimal conditions; He interrupted.

- **Nehemiah** wept over broken walls and couldn't ignore the burden (Nehemiah 1:4). His career pivoted because his spirit was stirred.
- **Esther** felt the nudge through Mordecai's challenge: *"Who knows whether you have come to the kingdom for such a time as this?"* (Esther 4:14, NKJV). She abandoned comfort for her calling.
- **Paul** was nudged on the Damascus Road—not gently, but purposefully. That nudge transformed persecution into proclamation.

Even Jesus felt the divine nudge to go to Jerusalem, knowing it would cost Him his life. The nudge is rarely easy, but it is always redemptive.

Recognizing Your Nudge

I know well the spiritual mechanics of divine discomfort: the sleepless nights over content that I needed to edit; the sudden urgency around a decision I postponed, like going to seminary; the conviction while reading Scripture, like it was speaking only to me.

The Whisper of Purpose

There are moments when something grips your spirit so tightly, you can't shake it—no matter how hard you try. It's not anxiety. It's not an impulse. It's a divine nudge. It sticks. It lingers. It whispers in the quiet corners of your day, "You won't feel settled until you act."

This is what happened to me one afternoon as I clocked out from my job to head home. I had this urge to call the seminary I had applied to a few years ago but hadn't enrolled in. The nudge became a pebble in my shoe, and so I put down my bag, found a Yellow Pages book (this was before Google), looked up the seminary number, and called. I was told by the admission's office that my application was scheduled to be shredded at the close of the business day if I did not reactivate it. For those who have gone through the process of applying to grad school, this is not a process you want to repeat. So, I asked if my application could remain open while I was still contemplating.

> *There are moments when something grips your spirit so tightly, you can't shake it*

These nudges build momentum. You'll hear a sermon, read a verse, or have a conversation—and suddenly, others unknowingly confirm what God has already whispered. It's as if heaven is echoing the invitation, layering grace upon grace. And though you may feel unqualified, you won't feel unsupported. Divine nudges come with provision. They don't manipulate; they invite. They don't coerce; they call. They are gentle but persistent, holy but human. They grip your peace, not to disturb it, but to redirect it.

A word of caution: Ignoring these nudges dims discernment. It dulls the spiritual ear and delays divine opportunities. The longer we resist, the harder it becomes to recognize the next whisper. Obedience sharpens clarity. Action unlocks the next step. The minute I took the step to enroll into seminary, clarity began to unfold. So if something is stirring—if a thought won't leave, if peace feels elusive, if confirmations keep showing up—pause. Listen. Ask. And then move. Because the nudge isn't just about you; it's about what God wants to do through you.

How Discomfort Reveals Divine Direction

Not every whisper comes with warmth. Some arrive like a restless stirring: a nudge to move, a shift in peace, a slow erosion of satisfaction in a place you once felt at home. It's uncomfortable, yet holy. Discomfort isn't always an enemy; sometimes it's a divine disruptor, used to disturb what no longer aligns with your calling.

> *Not every whisper comes with warmth. Some arrive like a restless stirring*

And yet, God never forces us to action. He uses nudges because He honors our free will and invites us into partnership, not coercion. Some examples of nudges include a call to leave a job, to reach out to someone, to start a ministry, or to step into unfamiliar territory. God uses discomfort to expand our capacity, deepen our trust, and sharpen our focus.

The Role of Holy Discontent

Holy discontent is the sacred dissatisfaction that stirs your soul. It's the feeling that something isn't right—and maybe you're the one called to change it.

Biblical examples include Moses, who was disturbed by the oppression of his people (Exodus 2:11–12); and Nehemiah, who was burdened by the broken walls of Jerusalem (Nehemiah 1:3–4).

Modern anecdotes of nudges are told by people who started nonprofits, church ministries, or movements because they couldn't ignore the need. This nudge led my husband and me to start a ministry that focused on enriching marriages and helping refugees from Africa find a place to connect.

Discontentment can act as a compass. What breaks your heart may be where your purpose begins. What things jump out to you as unfair? Where are you eager to see change? What can you do to begin walking in the direction of difference-making? Nudges are how God authors legacy. He doesn't shout your next chapter; He nudges it. Your purpose isn't discovered; it's responded to. Clarity often begins with discomfort, and a legacy of obedience is built one small yes at a time.

Discerning Divine Nudges: How to Tell the Difference

Not every stirring in the soul is sacred. Some are distractions. Some are fears dressed as urgency. But divine nudges carry a distinct fingerprint, one that can be tested and trusted. Here's how to tell the difference:

- **Does it align with Scripture?** God will never contradict His Word. A true nudge will echo the heart of Scripture, even if it challenges your comfort. It may stretch you, but it won't violate the truth. If the whisper leads you toward love, justice, humility, or obedience, it's worth leaning into.

- **Does it lead to clarity or confusion?** If the stirring leads to deeper trust, healing, or surrender, it's likely from God. If it breeds anxiety, shame, or confusion, pause and test it.
- **Does it draw you closer to God or isolate you?** God's voice always draws us near. Even when He convicts, He does so with the intent of communion. A true nudge will make you want to pray, seek, worship, or rest in His presence. If it pushes you into isolation, secrecy, or self-reliance, it may not be holy.

Trusted voices can help you interpret what you're sensing. Who around you is spiritually mature and can help you discern a possible nudge? Who has been nudged over and over again and been obedient to God? Seek such people out and get counsel.

To resist a divine nudge is not always a sin, but it often delays surrender. Jonah didn't reject God outright, but he ran. In his running, he found himself swallowed by a storm, then a fish, before yielding to the call (Jonah 1:1-17). His story reminds us that the cost of delay is often discomfort, confusion, or missed impact.

> *To resist a divine nudge is not always a sin, but it often delays surrender.*

We don't always say no to God. Sometimes we say, "Not yet." We justify our inaction with logic: "It doesn't make sense right now." (This was my logic because I was busy with work and church.) We hide behind prayer: "I'm still waiting for confirmation." We blame the schedule: "I'll do it when things slow down." But divine nudges don't submit to our timelines.

They are invitations to trust that God knows what He's doing, even when we don't. They ask us to move before we see the full map, to obey before we feel ready, to surrender before we understand.

Delay doesn't cancel the call, but it can complicate the journey. The longer we wait, the more tangled our path becomes. And yet, even in the detour, grace remains. God doesn't revoke the invitation; He simply waits for our yes. The example of King Saul comes to mind: His continual disobedience and doubt caused God to remove him from the throne and make David king.

So if you feel the nudge, don't wait for perfect clarity. Move with holy courage. Trust that obedience will bring understanding, not the other way around.

Responding to the Nudge

Once you recognize the nudge, the next step is obedience. But obedience often requires courage. Here is how you need to respond to the nudge:

- **Fear of stepping out:** You're frozen in fear. You are stuck asking, "What if I fail? What if I'm wrong? What if I'm not enough?" Just step out in faith.
- **Urge to run away:** Whatever God has told you, you're running in the other direction. Remember Jonah, and don't delay God's inevitable will.
- **Ignoring it:** You've been sensing that nudge, but you're resisting it. You're keeping busier than ever to drown out what you know is God nudging you. God often reveals the next step only after we take the first one.

- **Small steps:** You may not have taken a leap, but you're moving forward. You're taking one small step at a time.
- **Obedience over outcome:** Your job is to respond. God handles the results.
- **Acknowledgement:** You've written it down or spoken it aloud. Admit it's pressing, even if it's disruptive. *"Lord, I sense You calling me toward this. I don't feel ready, but I do feel stirred."*
- **Prayer:** You're talking to God about the nudge, asking Him to clarify your next step. Nudges rarely give the whole map, but they always light the next marker.
- **Counsel:** You've invited trusted spiritual voices (like your spiritual peers or ministry leaders) to help you discern the truth. Is this impulse rooted in ego or obedience?
- **Take one step of faith:** Don't try to leap; just move. Send the email. Make the call. Share the word. Trust that momentum follows movement. You can't have momentum until you are moving.

Nudged into the Unknown

You need to hear this: Nudges aren't reserved for prophets and pastors. They're for nurses in exam rooms, professors at podiums, parents at crosswalks, colleagues at work, and members in churches. Nudges find you wherever you are—quietly, persistently, purposefully. They lead you into unexpected places: a side conversation that heals someone's soul, a new role where your calling begins to flourish, or a decision that frees others to grow. Obeying the nudge may cost you comfort, but it restores clarity. It's the sacred *yes* that unlocks purpose.

What persistent nudge have you resisted? Perhaps it's a call to forgive, to speak, to rest, or to begin. Perhaps it's a shift in direction or a deepening of purpose. Whatever it is, its persistence is grace. The tap on the shoulder is confirmation that God is still pursuing, still inviting, still believing in your becoming. What would happen if you stopped resisting and simply said yes?

Testimonies of Nudged Obedience

I was nudged as a young woman in my twenties to consistently go and sit at the door of a human resources office in a hospital until the director gave me a patient transporter job. This job led me into the career of professional nursing and ultimately to being a professor in a graduate nursing program, where I still am today. Through my nursing and teaching careers, I have touched many lives by offering emotional support and compassion during difficult times, by being an advocate, and by driving innovations through project improvements and policy changes. I have been impacted by the connections I've made with my colleagues, my patients, and my students. I also feel gratified when my patients take an active role in their well-being and my students generate their own knowledge.

My daughter, after earning her first degree and working dissatisfying jobs, got the nudge to go to nursing school. Because she was not strong in the sciences, however, she hesitated. But after completing her prerequisite courses for nursing and repeating a few science courses, she was accepted to nursing school. Today she is a registered nurse, and all because she obeyed that divine nudge. Your greatest breakthroughs may be resting just on the other side of your next yes.

Prayer of Surrender

A prayer of surrender becomes our posture. I surrendered my desire for medical school and obeyed the nudge to go to nursing school. My redirection was not a defeat, but a release. We lay down our defenses, our plans, and our pride, and we open our hands to what God has been gently urging all along. This prayer is not always eloquent—it may be as simple as "Yes, Lord," or "I'm listening." In surrender, we stop kicking and start yielding. We trust that the One who calls us also guides us, and that obedience will lead us not into loss, but into life.

Reflection and Application

Scripture Focus: *"Whether you turn to the right or to the left, your ears will hear a voice behind you, saying, 'This is the way; walk in it.'"* (Isaiah 30:21, NIV)

Devotional Thought: The nudge is rarely convenient. It arrives as divine friction against comfort—sometimes disguised as restlessness, unease, or repeated promptings we'd rather ignore. But behind every nudge is the invitation to obey, to surrender, to trust. God guides not just in clarity but through persistent discomfort that directs us toward purpose. Holy nudges may challenge your timeline, but they never confuse God's intentions.

Questions for Reflection:

- Have you been sensing a nudge that you've been ignoring?
- What area of your life feels unsettled right now?
- What would it look like to take one small step of obedience?
- When was the last time a gentle prompt shifted your direction?
- How do you respond when obedience feels uncomfortable?
- What spiritual outcome has emerged from following divine interruptions?

Action Steps:

- Journal about a time you felt a divine nudge and what happened when you followed it.
- Identify one area where you feel holy discontentment, then pray for clarity.
- Share your nudge with a trusted friend or mentor for accountability.
- Write a list of the nudges you've sensed this year. Circle one that you haven't acted on.
- Commit to one step of obedience this week, then journal the outcome.

Prayer:

"God, give me the courage to respond to Your nudges. Even when I feel unprepared, help me to trust that You are guiding me. When I resist, lovingly press again. Teach me to honor the holy ache of divine nudging. Let my hesitation yield to obedience."

3

Discerning The Voice Within

Discerning the voice within is about spiritual attentiveness—the kind of listening that requires soul-tuning more than soundproof clarity.

This chapter invites you to

- reflect on the internal dialogue between fear, flesh, and faith.
- explore biblical examples like Elijah's whisper and David's heart.
- practice tuning your spiritual ear to recognize God's voice.
- surrender confusion and self-doubt.
- declare clarity and confidence in divine direction.

John 10:27 offers a tender assurance: "My sheep hear my voice, and I know them, and they follow me" (KJV). This verse speaks of intimacy, recognition, and relationship. It's not about mastering spiritual technique, but about belonging. The sheep do not strain to hear; they simply know the voice of the One who loves them.

Discerning the voice within requires a heart tuned to God's rhythm and a spirit quiet enough to hear Him speak. My heart tuned in as I lay awake in the middle of the night, trying to find answers about my next steps. I lay awake not because I didn't trust God but because my soul would not rest until I heard from Him.

Elijah learned this on the mountain, when God bypassed the wind, earthquake, and fire to speak through a gentle whisper (1 Kings 19:12). It was a lesson in spiritual sensitivity: God's voice isn't always dramatic, but it's always divine. David, too, modeled this discernment. His psalms reveal a heart that listened deeply, responded honestly, and waited patiently. Whether in triumph or turmoil, David's inner life was shaped by communion with God. Together, Elijah's whisper and David's heart taught me that the voice within isn't always loud, but when it's God, it's unmistakable. It speaks through conviction, peace, and holy tension, guiding us not by volume but by truth.

We live in a world filled with voices: loud ones, clever ones, urgent ones. Some are external, like media, culture, and expectations. Others are internal, like ambition, anxiety, memory, and longing. Somewhere in the swirl rests a quieter presence, the voice within, marked not by emotion or ego, but by the Spirit of God dwelling in us. In a world filled with competing sounds and spiritual static, this voice reminds us that God's voice is not distant or cryptic; it is familiar, personal, and consistent with His character.

The soul must be tuned into the right frequency to hear clearly. Just as a radio must be finely adjusted to catch the right signal, our souls must be attuned to the "divine wavelength." This tuning is not mechanical; it's relational. It involves quieting the noise, discerning the difference between fear and faith, and learning God's voice. The soul's frequency is best calibrated through presence, patience, and practice.

To discern the voice within is to untangle God's whisper from the world's noise and our own internal narrative. It's to sift through spiritual static and locate truth. This practice requires awareness, emotional maturity, and a listening posture. As I made my closet a sanctuary of quiet and an altar where I personally waited on God, I was able to hear words of hope and restoration, words like, "You are going to get through this."

What is the "Voice Within"?

The voice within is not merely our conscience, intuition, or personal feeling. It is the echo of the Spirit's indwelling presence (Romans 8:9), the internal resonance that confirms, convicts, or cautions—often before our mind can rationalize it. Jesus said, "My sheep hear My voice" (John 10:27, KJV)—not just externally, but internally. The Spirit testifies with our spirit (Romans 8:16, NIV), meaning that divine guidance can be experienced as an internal knowing, a sense of peace, a sudden conviction, or a sanctified unease. But this voice doesn't shout. It doesn't flatter. It rarely entertains. Instead, it guides.

One of the most challenging aspects of walking in purpose is learning to trust the voice within. But what happens when that voice is clouded by fear, insecurity, or past wounds? How do you know if it's God speaking or just your own thoughts?

Discerning the voice within is not about achieving perfection in hearing, but about cultivating sensitivity, trust, and spiritual maturity. To do this, I had to read and meditate on the word of God more. I had to pray more. I had to listen more. I had to make room to be alone and also to be with spiritual mentors.

We all have an internal narrative. It's the voice that speaks in our heads. Sometimes it encourages us; other times it criticizes, doubts, or second-guesses. Self-talk, though familiar, can be rooted in past trauma or lingering insecurity. It's often shaped by cultural expectations, the pressure of comparison, or the fear of failure. Sometimes it even sounds logical, reasonable, measured, and convincing. But logic alone doesn't guarantee spiritual truth. When self-talk lacks the anchoring voice of God, it can subtly steer us away from peace, purpose, and obedience. That's why discernment matters: tuning our hearts to recognize what is merely familiar versus what is divinely true.

The challenge is learning to recognize which voice is which. In short, these are the three voices we hear:

- God's voice: loving, guiding, convicting, never condemning
- Our voice: shaped by experience, emotion, and logic
- The enemy's voice: accusatory, fearful, confusing

Discerning the voices you hear isn't optional; it's sacred stewardship. No matter where you are in your spiritual journey, you have an impact on those in your circle of influence, and you need to be prepared to help others discern what they are hearing too.

> *Discerning the voice within is essential for spiritual maturity.*

Discerning the voice within is essential for spiritual maturity. It enables you to respond wisely to divine nudges, avoiding impulsive decisions that masquerade as inspiration. In my moments of emotional turmoil, discernment kept me grounded in God's truth, anchoring my responses in peace rather than reaction. Discernment equips us to lead others from a place of surrendered authority, not personal ambition. Without it, even gifted believers risk becoming driven instead of led, propelled by pressure rather than purpose. The inner voice we obey must be refined by truth, not filtered through trauma or shaped by worldly success.

Sorting Through the Inner Noise

You heard something: a thought, a prompting, a phrase that lingered longer than usual. But now you're second-guessing. *Was that God, or just me?*

Welcome to the battle of inner voices. We are deeply familiar with noise, but we're rarely trained to trust *discernment*.

Not every inner voice is divine. Scripture warns us of counterfeit promptings: desires masquerading as destiny, fear disguised as wisdom.

> *Not every inner voice is divine.*

Here's how you can begin to distinguish what's Spirit-led versus what's self-driven:

Source	Marker of Discernment	Evidence
Spirit	Peace, clarity, alignment with Scripture	Fruit of the Spirit (Galatians 5:22–23)
Flesh	Urgency, self-protection, emotional reward	Works of the flesh (Galatians 5:19–21)
Enemy	Confusion, condemnation, distraction	Distorts truth, divides purpose (John 10:10)

Does the internal voice you're hearing invite deeper trust or stir fear? Does it elevate the cross or feed the ego? That framework creates sacred filters. It's about tuning your ear, not to volume, but to tone. Consider the voice you're hearing. What words or phrases stand out? What feelings does it provoke?

If the voice is...	It may be...
Rushed, anxious, accusing	Fear or pressure
Gentle, firm, consistent	God's prompting
Circular, obsessed with control	Ego or insecurity
Loving, truthful, aligning	The Spirit's whisper

Discernment grows in stillness, not in striving.

Tools for Discernment

Discerning God's voice is a skill that can be developed. It requires intentionality, humility, and practice. Here are some tools to help you in the journey:

- **Scripture as the standard:** God will never contradict His Word. Knowing Scripture helps you recognize His voice.

- **Prayer and stillness:** Create space to listen, not just to speak.
- **Wise counsel:** Trusted mentors or spiritual leaders can help confirm what you're sensing.
- **Peace as a compass:** Colossians 3:15 says, "Let the peace of Christ rule in your hearts" (NIV).
- **Confirmation through circumstances:** These include open doors, divine timing, and repeated themes.

These tools take time and practice to implement. Don't rush discernment.

Overcoming Self-Doubt

Self-doubt is one of the most persistent barriers to hearing God clearly. It whispers lies like "You're not good enough," "You're probably wrong," and "Who do you think you are?" These voices often echo from past failures, fear of man, perfectionism, or a shaky sense of identity in Christ.

But God is not deterred by our uncertainty. He has a history of using the unsure: Moses, Gideon, and Jeremiah all wrestled with doubt, yet they were called and empowered for divine purpose. The way forward is to replace lies with truth. Speak Scripture over your life, practice gratitude and affirmation, and remember God's faithful track record. In doing so, clarity returns, and the voice of God rises above the noise.

When the Voice Within Is Divine

Like in any relationship, God's voice becomes clearer the more time we spend with Him. Discernment isn't a lightning strike;

it's a slow, sacred unfolding. Morning quiet times become altars of intimacy. Journaling what you sense God is saying turns fleeting impressions into lasting dialogue. Reflecting on past decisions reveals patterns of divine guidance, even in missteps. And yes, learning through trial and error is part of the process. God honors the heart that longs to obey, even when the steps are imperfect. Spiritual confidence is built not in grand gestures, but in celebrating small wins, like answered prayers, divine confirmations, and the quiet peace that follows obedience.

Then there are those unmistakable moments: A verse leaps from the page, echoing your thoughts. An urge to pray brings peace before you even know why. Your spirit leaps at a truth you couldn't have imagined alone. This is not mere intuition. It's the indwelling Presence. "The Spirit himself testifies with our spirit that we are God's children" (Romans 8:16, NIV). And when He speaks, we walk differently, think differently, obey differently.

> **God's voice becomes clearer the more time we spend with Him.**

Robertson (2011) defines the Latin phrase *Lectio Divina* as a practice of reading and meditating on Scripture that transforms one's life. *Lectio Divina* can be a sacred tool for this tuning. In this ancient practice, we don't just read Scripture; we listen to it. We linger over a passage, allowing it to speak to us in layers: reading, meditating, memorizing, praying, and contemplating. It's not about extracting information but receiving revelation. Through *Lectio*, we begin to notice which words stir us, which phrases comfort or convict, and how God might be speaking uniquely to our current season. It's a slow, sacred rhythm that trains our ears to recognize the Shepherd's voice.

Reflection and Application

Illustration: Picture a radio with static. Tuning in to the right frequency takes time, but once you find it, the message is clear.

Scripture Focus: *"My sheep listen to My voice; I know them, and they follow Me."* (John 10:27, NIV)

Devotional Thought: God's voice is not always dramatic; often, it's distinguishable only to those who've cultivated holy familiarity. Discernment isn't about detection; it's about devotion. The inner voice aligned with heaven's wisdom is shaped by Scripture, surrendered living, and spiritual maturity. The noise within us—fear, pride, assumptions—often masquerades as clarity. But God trains us to recognize His nudges through patterns of peace, gentle redirection, and a subtle unrest toward compromise.

Questions for Reflection:

- What voices are loudest in your life right now?
- When was the last time you felt confident that God spoke to you? What did His voice sound like?
- How have you distinguished between God's voice, your inner voice, and the enemy's voice?
- What practice helps you listen better?

Action Steps:

Below are various action steps you can take to strengthen your spiritual ear. Pick one or two to focus on this week.

- **Silence Practice**: Schedule five to ten minutes of daily silence. Let your soul breathe.

- **Scripture Anchoring**: Read with expectation for five to ten minutes a day. God speaks through His Word.
- **Journaling**: Track what you sense for a week. Notice the patterns that emerge.
- **Prayer Dialogue**: Talk with God, not at Him. Listen.
- **Write down** three lies you often believe about yourself and replace them with Scripture-based truths.
- **Ask God to confirm something** you've been unsure about, and be open to how He responds.
- **Retreat** from one distracting voice this week, such as media, comparison, or overplanning. Replace it with intentional listening, such as Scripture meditation or silent walks. Journal about the contrasting voices.

Prayer:

"Father, help me to discern Your voice above all others. Quiet my doubts and increase my faith to follow Your lead. Speak, Lord—not just so I hear, but so I obey. Train my heart to recognize Your tone in the quiet. Silence the counterfeit calls and draw me toward what only You would say."

4

Called But Not Yet Sent

If you have been called but not yet sent, you're in that in-between space where faith is forged and identity is refined.

This chapter invites you to

- reflect on seasons of preparation before public purpose.
- explore biblical examples like Moses in Midian, Joseph in prison, and Jesus in the wilderness.
- practice embracing the tension between calling and commissioning.
- surrender impatience and comparison.
- declare peace in the waiting and trust in divine timing.

Jeremiah 1:5 offers a profound glimpse into divine intentionality: "Before I formed you in the womb, I knew you…" (NIV). This verse is a declaration of preexistent purposes, a reminder that our lives are not accidents but intricately woven designs. Before action, there was a knowing. Before formation, there was intention. This sacred pause before release reveals a God who does not rush but prepares, who does not improvise but ordains. It invites us to honor the waiting seasons not as delays, but as divine incubation.

Being called but not yet sent is a sacred tension, a divine pause where preparation outweighs visibility. My calling happened at the age of twelve, but my sending was not until the age of thirty-four, when God opened the door for us to begin our own ministry in the city of Arlington, Texas.

Don't question your calling just because it's taking a long time to come to fulfillment. Moses spent forty years in Midian, tending sheep in obscurity after fleeing Egypt. Though the call to deliver Israel was already on his life, God used the desert to shape his humility, patience, and dependence.

Joseph, too, was called through dreams of leadership, yet he found himself confined in prison—forgotten by men but remembered by God. In that hidden place, his character was refined, and his gift of interpretation matured into the key that would unlock his destiny.

Jesus, freshly baptized and affirmed by the Father, was led into the wilderness—not to begin His ministry, but to be tested, strengthened, and prepared for it. Each of them carried a calling long before the platform appeared. Their waiting wasn't punishment; it was preparation. And in that holy delay, God was crafting vessels fit for the weight of purpose.

When I was twelve, a lady moved into my neighborhood and asked me to gather kids in the community for Bible story time. She told me there would be Kool-Aid and candies (I grew up in Liberia, West Africa, and this was the ideal snack that would draw all kids). With excitement, I gathered as many kids as I could, and the lady taught us stories from the Bible using flannelgraphs (Bible stories told in pictures). The following

Sunday, she asked me to gather the kids again, but this time she asked me to review the Bible story from the previous Sunday. It was the story of Joseph and his brothers, which I reviewed using the flannelgraphs.

From that Sunday on, I became her co-teacher. Most of the time, I reviewed the previous week's lesson, then held the pictures up while she taught that week's lesson. I also gave out prizes to kids who correctly answered questions. To this day, I love to give out prizes when I teach, whether at church or in academia. Even though I felt the call of God in my life at the age of twelve, like King David, my sending period would be years later.

Sacred Pause Before Release

A sacred pause before release evokes the image of a potter holding clay just before shaping or a conductor lingering over silence before the first note. Waiting is not passive; it is preparatory. It is the space where identity is clarified, where calling is refined, and where trust is deepened.

In this pause, God is forming something within us that cannot be rushed. The waiting becomes holy ground, where transformation is happening beneath the surface. There's a peculiar ache in purpose, the season between knowing you're called and being sent. It's the space between revelation and release. It feels like holy discomfort, like a readiness that hasn't yet met opportunity. And for many believers, especially those gifted, anointed, and affirmed, this season can feel more like delay than design.

But calling is not commissioning. And the time between the two is not punishment; it's preparation. When my husband and

I felt the nudge to start a church, our preparation time felt like punishment, but in hindsight, we know it was all preparatory.

Waiting with Intention

To be called is to receive divine assignment. It is God's declaration over your life, identity, and future. It's the burning bush moment, the Damascus encounter, the whispered *"You were made for this."* But to be *sent* is to be released into that assignment—with authority, timing, and alignment. Biblically, the gap between calling and sending is not uncommon:

> **To be called is to receive divine assignment. It is God's declaration over your life, identity, and future.**

- **Joseph** was called through dreams but sent only after betrayal, servitude, and imprisonment.
- **David** was anointed king as a boy but sent years later, after dodging spears, wandering in caves, and earning trust.
- **Jesus** Himself waited until age thirty to begin His public ministry, despite being the Word made flesh from birth.

The in-between is not spiritual limbo. It's holy tension designed to prepare the vessel for what the assignment demands. Waiting is not wasted time. In fact, it's often the most formative part of the journey. Many of the Bible's greatest leaders experienced long seasons of waiting between their calling and their commissioning.

To wait with intention is to resist the urge to fill the silence or force the outcome. It is to remain present, expectant, and open. This practice asks us to trust that God is working even when we cannot see it. It may involve journaling our longings, praying through uncertainty, or simply sitting in stillness. Waiting with intention is not about doing nothing; it's about doing the deep work of becoming. It's about aligning our pace with God's and allowing the forming to unfold.

Waiting seasons are not wasted; they are sacred classrooms where God teaches us to obey without applause, trust without clarity, and prepare without validation. In these quiet stretches, we learn to serve in obscurity, believe without a blueprint, and build discipline without a platform. I've seen this in both ministry and academia: students brimming with knowledge but lacking wisdom, preachers with eloquence but no maturity, practitioners with skill but no humility. The delay isn't denial; it's divine shaping. God is not just preparing the work; He's preparing the worker. In the silence, He is forming the kind of character that can carry the weight of calling.

> *To wait with intention is to resist the urge to fill the silence or force the outcome.*

Let's further consider the three examples of those who were called but not yet sent:

1. Gifted but Grounded (Genesis 37–41, NIV)

Joseph's dreams revealed greatness, but his journey included betrayal, slavery, false accusation, and prison. Only after he refined his dreams did Pharaoh declare, "Can we find anyone like this man, one in whom is the spirit of God?" (Genesis 41:38, NIV). Joseph was sent when his leadership could sustain the prophecy, not just interpret it.

2. Anointed but Hidden (1 Samuel 16, NIV)

David's anointing took place in the presence of his brothers, but his deployment was delayed. He returned to tending sheep, but the Spirit of the Lord rushed upon him from that moment forward. "Then Samuel took the horn of oil and anointed him…And the Spirit of the Lord rushed upon David" (1 Samuel 16:13, ESV). David didn't need the throne to begin stewarding his anointing. God was more concerned with his formation than his recognition.

3. Prepared in the Wilderness (Matthew 4, NIV)

Before Jesus preached, healed, or chose disciples, He was led into the wilderness for testing. His identity was affirmed—"This is My Son" (Luke 9:35, NIV)—but His commissioning required spiritual resistance and unwavering obedience. Sometimes God affirms us *before* He uses us publicly. The wilderness confirms whether we'll steward our calling when no one is watching.

The space between calling and commissioning is not a void. It's a forge. In that sacred in-between, God shapes spiritual maturity, teaching us to discern His voice rather than chase His plans. He cultivates emotional integrity by healing the insecurities that would otherwise sabotage destiny. He deepens relational wisdom, guiding us to build life-giving partnerships instead of chasing platforms. He instills a theology of process, where slow growth is not a setback but a strategy.

Navigating the Delay Without Resentment

Delay is rarely comfortable, and it often tempts us to take matters into our own hands. We rush ahead: "I'll make my own opportunity." We compare: "She's already speaking and I'm still serving." We doubt: "Maybe I misheard God." But resentment in the waiting only clouds discernment and corrodes trust. God's timing is not just about the destination; it's about the kind of person we become en route. The delay is not a detour; it's a design. It teaches us to steward obscurity, honor others' pace, and anchor our identity in God's voice rather than visible progress. To navigate the delay well, we must return to intimacy: daily quiet, honest journaling, and remembering the confirmations that first called us. The waiting is not passive; it's formative. And when the time comes, the vessel will be ready not just to carry the message, but to embody it.

Delay is divine when you are surrendered. Here are some posture shifts for you as you read on:

1. **Rest in the reveal**. Being *called* is sacred. Don't rush to prove it. Sit with the revelation. Let it grow inside of you before you showcase it. *"The vision awaits its appointed time… If it seems slow, wait for it"* (Habakkuk 2:3, ESV).
2. **Prepare like you're sent**. You don't need an audience to study, pray, rehearse, or grow. Preparation *before* release is what ensures sustainability after. *"Study to show thyself approved…"* (2 Timothy 2:15, KJV).
3. **Honor the quiet**. Obscurity doesn't mean insignificance. The cave seasons produce prophets. The margins birth reformers. You may be teaching five students now, but those five could become apostles, innovators, or intercessors later. Every "small" assignment is sacred (Zech. 4:10). The sent season will come (Habakkuk 2:3).

Waiting can be painful, especially when you see others stepping into their purpose while you feel stuck in the shadows. The frustration is real, and comparison only sharpens the sting. Social media showcases highlight reels, while your timeline feels slow, hidden, and unfinished. But purpose isn't a race; it's a journey uniquely designed by God. Some of our friends in the same church we were attending were starting their ministry and asked us to join them, but we never felt the nudge to stop serving in our current church. So we kept serving where we were planted until God said, "It's time to start your own ministry to serve another group of people," people who couldn't be reached in that current location. Trusting God for your journey means resisting the urge to measure your progress against someone else's.

Sometimes doubt creeps in when we wait too long: "Did I hear God wrong? Am I doing something wrong?" These questions are not signs of failure; they're invitations to deeper intimacy.

> **Purpose isn't a race; it's a journey uniquely designed by God.**

Even biblical heroes wrestled with delay. Abraham's detour with Hagar reminds us of the danger of forcing God's promise (Gen. 16:1–6). Premature promotion may look appealing, but it often comes at the cost of character, clarity, and peace.

Still, God is faithful to leave signs along the path. Encouragement from others, opportunities to grow in your gifting, and a deepening burden for your calling are subtle confirmations that you're not forgotten. And in the waiting, spiritual fruit begins to bloom—peace that surpasses understanding settles in, growth in wisdom abounds, and a quiet confidence that God is still writing your story deepens.

Living Fully While Waiting

God's silence isn't rejection; it's root work. In the quiet, He's deepening your foundation, anchoring your faith, and preparing you for the weight of what's ahead. Waiting doesn't mean doing nothing. It means doing the next right thing, with faithfulness and joy.

Serve where you are. David served Saul long before he wore a crown. Jesus honored His family by working as a carpenter before launching His ministry. Grow where you're planted. Use this time to study, train, and build habits that will sustain you when the pace quickens. Be faithful in the small, because as Luke 16:10 reminds us, whoever is faithful in little will be faithful in much.

When God sends, He sends with precision. He opens doors no man can shut (Revelation 3:8), aligns timing, resources, and support, and releases you with authority. And here's the beauty: He never sends you alone. Every sending comes with fresh anointing, angelic help, and divine favor.

Being sent doesn't mean the preparation ends; it means it transforms into stewardship. You'll still be learning, surrendering, listening. But the clarity of release confirms what the calling began. The waiting was never wasted; it was the womb of your becoming.

> *Being sent doesn't mean the preparation ends; it means it transforms into stewardship.*

So we ask, What is forming in the waiting? Perhaps it's courage, clarity, compassion, or conviction. Perhaps it's a new vision, a deeper surrender, or a quiet strength. Whatever it is, the waiting is not wasted. When the time comes, what emerges will bear the mark of divine craftsmanship. My preparation, which started at the age of twelve, allowed me to serve in various capacities while I waited to be sent into ministry.

Reflection and Application

Illustration: Think of a seed planted in the soil. It's called to be a tree, but it must first grow roots in the dark before breaking through the surface.

Scripture Focus: *"But the Lord said to me, 'Do not say, "I am a youth," for you shall go to all to whom I send you.'"* (Jeremiah 1:7, NKJV)

Devotional Thought: Being called is a promise; being sent is a posture. The waiting between these two is not wasted—it's strategic. God prepares character before visibility and depth before delivery. In the stillness, He removes ego, sharpens clarity, and hides you until timing aligns with obedience. You're not sidelined—you're sanctified. Jesus spent thirty quiet years before three loud ones. You're in holy company.

Questions for Reflection:

- What has God spoken to you about your calling?
- How have you seen growth in your waiting season?
- Are there areas where you've been tempted to rush ahead?
- What season of "almost" have you mistaken for abandonment?
- Where is God refining your readiness before release?
- How does private obedience prepare you for public impact?

Action Steps:

- Create a timeline of your calling: what you've heard, felt, and resisted.
- Mark where waiting has deepened your walk. Share one insight with a trusted mentor.
- Pray for patience and clarity, asking God to help you trust His timing.

Prayer:

"Lord, help me to trust your timing. Even when I feel ready, remind me that You are preparing me for something greater. Lord, don't rush me into visibility before I'm rooted in intimacy. Let waiting be worship. Shape me in silence so that when I'm sent, it's Your echo, not my ambition, that shines forth."

5

Purpose In Pieces

Purpose in pieces carries both the ache of fragmentation and the beauty of redemption.

This chapter invites you to

- reflect on fragmented experiences that feel disconnected.
- explore biblical examples like Ruth's journey, Nehemiah's rebuilding, and Peter's restoration.
- practice connecting life's broken pieces to a greater purpose.
- surrender the need for immediate understanding.
- declare faith that God is weaving wholeness from every part.

As Romans 8:28 reminds us, "And we know that in all things God works for the good of those who love him, who have been called according to his purpose" (NIV). This verse offers a lens of redemption, assuring us that even the fragmented, painful, or confusing moments are being gathered into something meaningful. It's not that every experience is inherently good, but that God is actively working through each one for a greater purpose.

Purpose doesn't always arrive whole—it often comes in fragments, scattered across seasons of loss, rebuilding, and redemption. Ruth's journey began in grief, walking away from everything familiar, yet each step toward Bethlehem was a piece of divine alignment. Her loyalty and quiet faith positioned her in the lineage of Christ. Nehemiah saw ruins, not revival, when he returned to Jerusalem. But through prayer, planning, and perseverance, he gathered the broken stones and rebuilt what others had abandoned; his purpose was forged in the rubble. Peter, once bold and brash, found himself shattered by denial. Yet on the shore, with Jesus cooking breakfast, restoration came gently. His failure wasn't the end; it was the beginning of a calling to shepherd others. Together, their stories remind us that purpose isn't always revealed in a single moment—it's assembled in pieces, often through pain, always through grace.

Within our first year of the ministry, God had opened doors for us to get started, but we also began facing major challenges with some of the members. I started questioning my calling and commissioning, but God reminded me again that because He was the one who called me, He would work out all things for my good, and twenty-eight years later, the ministry continues.

There were so many broken pieces in the first few years of the ministry that only God could have brought purpose to them. For example, God revealed the purpose for the conflict in the first year of the church's inception as a way to bring us into alignment with what He was doing and who He wanted in the leadership, but it was painful to see friends separate from us and the ministry we felt called to begin together. The revealed purpose was that we would fully depend on God to grow the ministry, not on friends. The problem with depending on friends and family is that it sometimes leads you away from purpose.

For many, the concept of purpose feels like a singular, shining destination. But for me, purpose often came not as a beam of light, but as fragments scattered across seasons, relationships, and revelations. These fragments, though disjointed at times, carried the fingerprints of divine intention. They were pieces of a larger mosaic. They all worked together to bring about purpose.

Purpose rarely enters fully formed. It emerges, often quietly, through moments that seem insignificant until seen in retrospect: the job you almost didn't take, the person who said a single word that stirred something eternal in you, the closed door that felt like rejection but rerouted your heart to fertile ground.

> **Purpose rarely enters fully formed. It emerges, often quietly, through moments that seem insignificant until seen in retrospect.**

Sometimes we treat calling as a clean equation: desire + talent + opportunity = destiny. But what if the very things you've wanted to leave out—the broken seasons, the long detours, the missteps—are the pieces God wants to use? Your calling isn't built in spite of your story, but *through* it.

This chapter will help you to trace the mosaic of your life. To see redemption in things you thought were wasted. To believe that God doesn't discard your hard chapters; He incorporates them.

Mosaic of Meaning

A mosaic is composed of broken pieces, shards of glass, bits of tile, fragments that once were discarded. Yet in the hands of an artist, these pieces are arranged into a stunning image. Our lives mirror this process. The heartbreaks, transitions, delays, and unexpected turns are not wasted. They are the raw materials of a masterpiece. What once felt like chaos to me has now become clarity. What seemed like a mess is now a message.

Scripture affirms this fragmented unfolding. In Acts 9, Saul's dramatic encounter on the Damascus road seemed like a flash of divine interruption, but his transformation into Paul and his purpose in ministry unfolded in pieces. Time in Arabia, years of preaching and persecution, and letters written from prison were all fragmented. His calling was not an instant certainty but a divine layering. Likewise, our purpose isn't revealed all at once. It's progressive. It's pieced together over time with threads of obedience, resilience, and grace.

> *The heartbreaks, transitions, delays, and unexpected turns are not wasted.*

We often expect purpose to follow a clear path: discover your calling, pursue it, succeed. But real life is messier. There are detours, delays, and disappointments. And yet, God is present in all of it.

> *But real life is messier. There are detours, delays, and disappointments.*

Clarity in the Fragments

It's tempting to minimize the value of small assignments, the shadowed seasons of "waiting" or "wandering." But these are often the refining crucibles where clarity is carved. My assignment started with just holding up Bible story images and having kids yell out the answers. Elijah's fiery call was preceded by hidden preparation. Ruth's destiny unfolded as she gleaned in fields behind harvesters. Peter lived most of his life as a fisherman, only to become the rock Jesus built His church on. When we pause to reflect, we find that each fragment holds value. The broken pieces—the seasons of disappointment, doubt, or detour—don't negate purpose; they deepen it. Like stained glass, the light of revelation only comes when the broken is bound together, reimagined by the hands of the Artist.

> *The seasons of disappointment, doubt, or detour—don't negate purpose; they deepen it.*

We often grow up under the illusion that life should follow a straight path—one marked by clarity, milestones, and predictable progress. Cultural voices urge us to "have it all figured out," as if certainty were a badge of honor. This pressure can be suffocating, especially when we find ourselves in seasons that don't match the timelines we once imagined. The anxiety of not being where we thought we'd be professionally, relationally, and spiritually can feel like failure.

But God rarely works in straight lines. His way is often winding, marked by detours that deepen our trust and

> *God rarely works in straight lines.*

pauses that refine our purpose. What feels like delay may be divine preparation. What seems like confusion may be sacred reorientation. In the kingdom, the journey itself is formative. The winding path is not a mistake; it's the invitation. Yes, there were a lot of winding paths in my life, some of which are narrated in the beginning of this book and the others of which are spread throughout this writing, so please don't miss them.

Biblical examples consistently affirm a piecewise unveiling of divine intent. Joseph's journey from pit to palace was marked by fragmented trials that culminated in national redemption. Esther began as an orphan in exile and her rise climaxed with royal courage. Moses wandered forty years before his purpose as a deliverer became clear.

God's sovereignty doesn't ignore the pieces; it orchestrates them. As we read at the start of this chapter, Romans 8:28 reminds us that "we know that all things work together for good…"(NKJV). Not just the visible victories, but the aching silences and the uncelebrated steps. Purpose, in God's economy, is cumulative. Every piece counts.

The quiet nudges, the momentary encounters, the shifts in strategy—these are echoes of a plan that unfolds with time. Isaiah 58:12 says, "You shall raise up the foundations of many generations; you shall be called the Repairer of the Breach…" (ESV). That's purpose. It's not self-contained. It doesn't live in isolation. It connects. It heals. It builds generational bridges from one faithful fragment to the next.

So, what brings these pieces together?

- **Obedience**: the thread that weaves purpose without full understanding

- **Reflection**: the mirror that shows where the pieces belong
- **Community**: the witness that affirms our alignment
- **Grace**: the adhesive that binds it all

There will always be days when the puzzle looks incomplete, when certain seasons feel wasted or unnecessary. But that's where faith lives—in trusting the unseen Hand that's still forming the masterpiece.

The Power of Redemption

We all carry moments we wish we could erase: failures, losses, and detours. Shame tempts us to stay silent, to believe that our past disqualifies us from purpose. But grace tells a different story. Grace doesn't just forgive; it restores. In God's hands, nothing is wasted.

Your pain becomes someone else's hope. The very places where you've been broken become bridges for others to cross. Your failure becomes wisdom, a lantern for those still walking through the dark. And your detour becomes direction, an unexpected route that leads to deeper trust and clearer calling. Take, for example, a detour during a road construction or an accident that takes you into unfamiliar neighborhoods just to get you back on track for your trip. It might take you longer to get to your destination, but these detours are necessary for your safety and for your journey to continue.

> *Your pain becomes someone else's hope.*

Scripture is full of divine recycling. Paul, once a persecutor of the church, became a voice to both Jews and Gentiles. His past gave him access and authority in places others couldn't reach.

Ruth's story, marked by loss and displacement, became a legacy of redemption that led to the lineage of Christ. These aren't just ancient stories; they're patterns of grace. Redemption doesn't erase the past; it reclaims it. Your story, with all its jagged edges, is not a liability; it's a testimony. And in the hands of a redeeming God, it qualifies you to speak, to lead, to love.

Gratitude Mapping

Gratitude mapping is a practice that helps us trace this mosaic of meaning. It invites us to reflect on fragmented memories and uncover the hidden gifts within them. By naming moments

> *Your story, with all its jagged edges, is not a liability; it's a testimony.*

of loss, surprise, or transformation and identifying what they taught us, we begin to see how each piece fits into the larger design. This is not just an exercise in thankfulness; it's a spiritual act of redemption, a way of reclaiming our story and recognizing God's artistry in it.

For me, gratitude mapping began with anchoring my reflections in the awareness of divine goodness—that is, knowing that God is good all of the time. I am grateful for the people who have shaped my journey, such as my family, my friends, my mentors, my colleagues, my neighbors, my church, my students, and even those who considered themselves my enemies. I'm thankful for the places that have held sacred meaning, like the prayer room at my church, my writing pad, my classrooms, and retreat centers. I'm thankful for the moments when God whispered clarity, breakthrough, and quiet joy. I am grateful for the growth I've achieved and the lessons I've learned through my pain and waiting, as well as the courage I've gained in obedience. I honor the many provisions from God, recognizing unexpected resources, sustaining grace, and open doors. And finally, I affirm legacy—the lives that have crossed my path, the seeds I've planted, and the stories that continue to unfold.

Looking back often reveals what we couldn't see in the moment. The job I hated taught me resilience. The heartbreaks taught me compassion and empathy. The delays taught me trust. Now I am able to connect the dots and see the purpose in my disappointments and pain.

Consider a time that felt like failure but led to unexpected growth in you. Recall a relationship that ended, yet opened space for healing. Reflect on a detour that brought clarity or a season of silence that deepened your listening. These moments, though once painful or confusing, may now shine with purpose. They are the tesserae of your mosaic—the small, sacred pieces that together reveal the image of a life shaped by grace.

The Power of Hindsight

Ten years into ministry, I could not see the way forward from all the hurts, the disappointments, and what seemed like punishments at the time. I realize now that sometimes clarity comes with hindsight. Journaling my journey allows me to trace the fingerprints of God across my story, to notice patterns, themes, and divine appointments that once felt random. What seemed ordinary has become sacred in retrospect. Skills developed in "random" jobs, relationships that shape character, and unexpected lessons all begin to reveal a deeper design.

Purpose is often hidden in the mundane. And when you begin to own your story—not just the polished parts but the broken pieces too—something powerful happens: You give others permission to do the same.

Authenticity is far more compelling than perfection. People connect with your scars, not your mask. I had to take off my mask and let church members see my hurt. I had been taught by seasoned pastors' wives and church leaders that sharing my pain and disappointments with church folks would put the ministry at risk. I realize now that vulnerability builds bridges that performance never could.

> *Purpose is often hidden in the mundane.*

My story is my superpower; no one else has lived my life, and my unique perspective is needed in the world. Living from wholeness means embracing your past as part of your purpose. It means walking in freedom and confidence, knowing that nothing is wasted and everything can be redeemed. When you stop hiding, you start healing, and you become a living invitation for others to do the same.

> *People connect with your scars, not your mask.*

I began to heal when I stopped hiding my pain and began sharing with those who held me close to heart. James 5:16 says, "Confess your faults one to another, and pray one for another, that ye may be healed…" (KJV). I believe many people in the church today remain in bondage and continue to be burdened because of the

> *Vulnerability builds bridges that performance never could.*

fear of being vulnerable. As a pastor's wife, sharing my pain with fellow believers and church leaders was a difficult call to make, but my healing depended on it. I traded my shame and pain for the joy of the Lord.

Purpose as Art, Not Architecture

Too often, we look for blueprints when God is assembling a mosaic. We want diagrams, timelines, and certainty. But perhaps the deepest purpose is not found in completed plans, but in yielded pieces, held loosely, surrendered joyfully. Jesus said in John 12:24, "Unless a kernel of wheat falls to the ground and dies, it remains only a single seed"(NIV). In purpose, sometimes clarity does not lead the way, but doubt does. Pieces such as your self-worth or your career may fall, but they also resurrect in purpose.

> *When you stop hiding, you start healing.*

My journey as a wife, mother, nurse, family nurse practitioner, educator, counselor, mentor, author, and spiritual guide is a piecewise unfolding. Every patient I have cared for and treated, every course I've taught, every student I've challenged, every client I've counseled, every young woman I've mentored, every devotional I've taught, every prayer I've whispered—they are all fragments, but together they form a powerful purpose. Not perfect. Not predictable. But profoundly pieced together by grace.

Reflection and Application

Illustration: A mosaic is made of broken tiles, yet when arranged with care, it becomes a beautiful work of art—just like our lives in God's hands.

Scripture Focus: *"And we know that in all things God works for the good of those who love Him, who have been called according to His purpose."* (Romans 8:28, NIV)

Devotional Thought: We often search for purpose like it's a singular destination. But God frequently reveals it in pieces: painful transitions, surprising shifts, and delayed clarity. Fragmentation is not failure; it's formation. Every season, even the ones we'd rewrite, is a brushstroke in the masterpiece. The challenge is not to see the whole but to trust the One who's crafting it.

Questions for Reflection:

- What parts of your story have you tried to hide or forget?
- Can you identify a moment that felt meaningless then but makes sense now?
- How do you see God bringing pieces of your story together now?
- What fragment of your life might hold a hidden purpose?
- Who has been a whisper of encouragement?

Action Steps:

- Create a "life timeline" marking key events, both painful and joyful: transitions, losses, and breakthroughs. Label

where you now see purpose revealed. Pray over the revelations yet to unfold.
- Write a letter to your younger self, affirming how far you've come.
- Share a piece of your story with someone who needs encouragement.

Prayer:

"God, thank You for using every part of my story. Help me to see purpose in the pieces and trust that nothing is wasted. Teach me to honor each shard as sacred. Let my scattered moments echo Your sovereignty."

6

Permission To Obey

Permission to obey isn't just about readiness; it's about release.

This chapter invites you to

- reflect on areas where you've delayed obedience to procure others' approval.
- explore biblical examples like Mary, Abraham, and Noah.
- practice naming areas where obedience has been postponed.
- surrender fear of judgment.
- declare spiritual permission for the next step.

Galatians 5:1 declares, "It is for freedom that Christ has set us free. Stand firm, then, and do not let yourselves be burdened again by a yoke of slavery" (NIV). This verse reframes obedience not as restriction, but as liberation. In Christ, we are not merely freed from sin—we are freed for something: for love, for purpose, for wholehearted yeses. True freedom is not the absence of boundaries but alignment with God's will. It is the ability to choose obedience without fear, shame, or hesitation.

Obedience to God rarely comes with full clarity; it only comes with permission. Mary received hers through a divine interruption: "Let it be to me according to your word" (Luke 1:38, NKJV). Her yes wasn't passive; it was powerful, spoken in the face of uncertainty, scandal, and awe. Abraham's permission came as a call to leave everything familiar and walk toward a promise he couldn't yet see (Genesis 12:1). His obedience wasn't rooted in understanding; it was anchored in trust. And Noah, asked to build an ark before a single drop of rain fell, obeyed not because it made sense, but because God had spoken (Genesis 6:22). Each of them teaches us that obedience doesn't wait for comfort or consensus; it begins when we accept that God's whisper is enough. Permission to obey is not granted by circumstances; it's birthed in surrender.

Choosing Faith over Validation

"Obedience" is a word that echoes deeply in Scripture: reverent, weighty, and often misunderstood. In a world that celebrates autonomy and self-expression, obedience can sound archaic, even oppressive. But spiritual obedience is not slavery; it's freedom. It's not restraint; it's release. It's not passivity; it's boldness. To obey the whisper of God is to walk in the direction of destiny, even when the roadmap is unclear and the surrounding voices grow loud.

For many believers, however, obedience is blocked not by rebellion but by the absence of permission from others. We wait for affirmation. We seek validation. And somewhere in the waiting, divine instruction gets muted by human delay. What if the real courage

> *Divine instruction gets muted by human delay.*

required in following Christ isn't hearing His voice, but granting ourselves permission to obey?

There comes a moment when what God asks of you won't make sense to everyone else. The alignment will cost you applause. The obedience may look like disobedience to those who don't hear what you hear. And that's where courage is forged: not in big acts, but in brave agreements. You don't need permission to obey what God already made clear. You need boldness to walk it out, even—or especially—when you walk alone.

The Myth of Readiness

"I'll obey when I'm ready." This was always my excuse. This myth is a familiar mantra among those facing spiritual decisions. But readiness, in the biblical sense, is rarely synonymous with comfort or certainty. Moses didn't feel ready to confront Pharaoh. Esther wasn't groomed to speak on behalf of her people in front of the king. Jeremiah resisted his call based on age. Mary said yes to a divine assignment that defied cultural norms and personal plans. Scripture is full of individuals whose obedience was preceded not by readiness but by revelation. They obeyed not because they felt equipped, but because they trusted the One who called them.

Obedience begins when we reject the myth that readiness is a prerequisite for obedience. Sometimes God speaks before we feel strong. Sometimes He instructs before we feel worthy. Obedience starts with a yes, even if it's a trembling one.

> *Obedience starts with a yes.*

The Paralysis of Approval

We live in a culture that conditions us to seek approval before proceeding. Social media reinforces this through likes, shares, and affirmation loops. Professional spaces require credentials, letters, and committee approvals. Even ministry can be bogged down by gatekeepers and hierarchy. Approval feels good; it affirms our choices and gives us a sense of belonging. But when approval is a requirement for obedience, it becomes a prison.

> *When approval is a requirement for obedience, it becomes a prison.*

Spiritual obedience isn't governed by the approval of others; it's propelled by intimacy. In Galatians 1:10, Paul makes a bold declaration: "Am I now trying to win the approval of human beings, or of God? ... If I were still trying to please people, I would not be a servant of Christ" (NIV). Obedience doesn't wait for applause. Obedience means walking in alignment with God's calling, even if it's misunderstood. It means serving in places not recognized by titles. It means ministering without needing a microphone. It means praying without posting.

When we anchor our obedience to God's voice rather than human affirmation, we unlock a new authority: an authority rooted in heaven. In our society today, approval is currency. From social media likes to family expectations, we're conditioned to seek validation before we act. But when God calls you to something, He doesn't always send a crowd to cheer you on. Sometimes, obedience means walking alone.

> *We often crave consensus because of a deep-rooted fear of rejection.*

For those in education, healthcare, or spiritual leadership, this identity as an obedient servant–leader is pivotal. You teach not because it's easy, but because obedience is your offering. You write not to gain applause, but to steward revelation. You counsel not from perfection, but from submission.

We often crave consensus because of a deep-rooted fear of rejection, a longing for affirmation, and the cultural conditioning that teaches us to "fit in" rather than stand out. These impulses, while human, can quietly steer us toward people-pleasing behaviors that carry significant spiritual and personal risks. When we prioritize approval over authenticity, our convictions become diluted, our obedience to God's promptings is delayed, and our attention drifts from the unique calling placed on our lives. Paul's question in Galatians 1:10 (NIV)—"Am I now trying to win the approval of human beings, or of God?"— invites us to examine whose voice we're truly listening to and whose approval we're ultimately seeking.

Obedience as Liberation

Obedience invites us to see surrender not as confinement, but as release. Like a bird freed from a cage, obedience allows us to soar into the life we were created for. It breaks the chains of people-pleasing, perfectionism, and paralysis. When we obey God, we are not losing autonomy; we are reclaiming our identity. We are stepping into the spacious place of trust, where saying yes becomes an act of courage and joy.

As a pastor's wife, I experienced this in a season of pain and isolation. I found it difficult to share my pain without being judged, which kept me in bondage. While ministry has its ups and downs, sometimes the "downs" were caused by people I love. When a member gravely offended me in a way that left me broken, it became a personal burden because sharing my pain required offering details that I did not wish to share. While Scripture encourages us to "confess your sins to each other and pray for each other so that you may be healed" (James 5:16, NIV), I felt that I was carrying the burden of the offense alone, even though I was the offended. So I suffered in silence for a long time. To be liberated, I had to obey the whisper to share this burden with a few trusted persons.

For the believer, obedience is not just an act; it's part of identity. In John 14:15, Jesus said, "If you love me, keep my commands" (NIV). Obedience flows from love, not legalism. The apostle Paul defines legalism in Colossians 2:20–23 as the dangers of following human-made rules, which appear wise but are ultimately ineffective in stopping the indulgence of the flesh and have no value in stopping the indulgence of sin. It's relational, not robotic. It's the child responding to a parent's voice not from fear, but from trust. That trust must include trusting ourselves to respond. We are not machines awaiting commands; we are co-laborers with Christ, empowered by the Holy Spirit to discern, respond, and act. This means choosing to obey is an act of spiritual maturity. It's saying, "I know the Shepherd's voice, and I trust what I'm hearing."

> *For the believer, obedience is not just an act; it's part of identity.*

The Cost of Delayed Obedience

Delayed obedience isn't neutral; it's costly. When we hesitate to act on what God has revealed, the ripple effects extend beyond ourselves. Delayed obedience costs us opportunities, divine encounters, and legacy. The story of Jonah reflects this vividly: His reluctance to obey not only led to personal upheaval but affected the lives of others aboard the ship. It took a storm, a fish, and a prayer for Jonah to realign. Giving ourselves permission to obey means moving before we're "swallowed." It means trusting that what God revealed was meant to be acted on, not filed away.

> *Delayed obedience isn't neutral; it's costly.*

God's instructions don't always make sense to others. In fact, they often challenge the status quo. Obedience often looks foolish before it looks faithful. When others don't understand, you're not obligated to explain what God has made clear to you. Obedience is your responsibility, not their understanding.

> *Obedience often looks foolish before it looks faithful.*

One of the greatest obstacles to obedience is the fear of rejection—the nagging worry about what others might think. Thoughts like "What if they think I'm crazy?" or "What if I lose relationships?" or even "What if I fail publicly?" can paralyze us before we ever take a step of faith. But fear is a poor guide for a life rooted in trust. Even Jesus faced rejection: His own family didn't believe in Him at first (John 7:5), and throughout His ministry, He was misunderstood, mocked, and ultimately crucified. Rejection, then, is not always a sign that we're wrong; it may be a sign that we're walking in truth.

Obedience requires courage, not because the path is always difficult, but because it's often lonely. The call to follow God's voice may lead us away from the crowd, away from comfort, and into a place where affirmation is scarce. That's why it's essential to give yourself permission to obey. Practically, this begins with a shift in mindset: recognizing that your worth is not tied to approval and that obedience is an act of trust, not performance. It means rehearsing truth over fear, surrounding yourself with voices that affirm your calling, and remembering that faithfulness is often quiet, unseen, and misunderstood.

Here are three spiritual strategies to keep in mind:

1. **Silence the inner critic**. The voice that says, "You're not ready," "You're not holy enough," or "You'll mess it up" must be silenced by truth. Replace it with Scripture, affirmation, and counsel.
2. **Write the vision, then walk it**. Habakkuk 2:2 reminds us to "write down the revelation and make it plain" (NIV). Clarity sometimes comes after movement. Don't wait to act until everything is mapped out.
3. **Seek spiritual witnesses, not validators**. Surround yourself with people who listen, pray, and confirm without trying to control. Spiritual witnesses point to God; validators focus on credentials.

Obedience often begins in the small, quiet moments, the ones that seem insignificant but shape the posture of our hearts. It looks like saying no when it would be easier to say yes. It means speaking truth even when silence feels safer and trusting that clarity and courage honor God more than comfort. And it's taking the first step of faith when the entire path isn't visible, believing that obedience doesn't require full understanding, just a willing heart. These small acts of obedience build spiritual muscle, preparing us for greater assignments and deeper trust.

God honors obedience. He provides strength, confirmation, and provision along the way. There's a deep freedom that comes when you stop living for the approval of others and start living for the audience of One. Obedience brings peace, even when it's hard, because there's a deep sense of alignment with God. Obedience builds trust, and every yes strengthens your confidence in giving the next one. Obedience leaves a legacy, and your courage can inspire others to follow God boldly. Not every act of obedience will be seen, but heaven records the quiet yes. Whether it's teaching a class, writing a chapter, or praying through the night, every yes is a seed planted.

> *Obedience often begins in the small, quiet moments.*

Throughout Scripture, we encounter individuals who moved forward, not because they were publicly affirmed or institutionally endorsed, but because they carried a quiet, resolute sense of divine permission. Their obedience wasn't contingent on comfort, consensus, or credentials; it was rooted in trust. Noah received no vote of confidence, no committee approval. He was given a command to build, and he obeyed, hammering out faith plank by plank while enduring ridicule from those who couldn't see what he saw.

David was chosen long before he was qualified by earthly standards. He didn't wait for a title to validate his calling. Instead, he stepped into obedience with a shepherd's heart and a warrior's courage, trusting that God's anointing preceded human recognition. Hannah, in a moment of profound surrender, offered her son Samuel to the Lord before there was even a temple to prepare him. Her obedience wasn't just personal; it unlocked a prophetic legacy that would shape the spiritual trajectory of a nation. Each of these lives whispers the same truth: Divine permission often comes before public affirmation. And when it does, it invites us to walk forward—not with certainty of the outcome, but with confidence in the One who calls.

Declaration Journaling

Declaration journaling can be a powerful practice in this space. By writing statements like "I am free to obey…," we begin to name and claim the permissions we've long withheld. These declarations might include "I am free to obey without needing approval," "I am free to obey even when I feel afraid," or "I am free to obey because God's voice is trustworthy." This form of journaling is both expressive and formative. It reshapes our inner narrative and reinforces the truth of our spiritual freedom.

> *Divine permission often comes before public affirmation.*

"Whose permission do you need to say yes?" invites honest introspection. Perhaps you need permission to disappoint others, to take a risk, to start small, or to let go of

> *I am free to obey*

control. Maybe you need to hear that you are already equipped, already loved, already called. Whatever the barrier, Christ's freedom dismantles it. More than simply allowed to obey, you are empowered to. And in that yes, you will find the spaciousness of grace.

Reflection and Application

Illustration: Imagine standing at a fork in the road, with a crowd urging you one way and a quiet voice calling you another. Obedience often means walking alone toward the quiet voice.

Scripture Focus: *"Do whatever He tells you."* (John 2:5, NIV)

"Am I now trying to win the approval of human beings, or of God?" (Galatians 1:10, NIV)

Devotional Thought: Sometimes the greatest barrier to obedience isn't a lack of clarity, but a lack of permission. We wait for signs, confirmations, and approvals, but heaven's nudge already carries divine consent. There is no need to negotiate what's already been affirmed. When Mary spoke at the wedding in Cana, she didn't know the full plan, but she understood the power of obedience. Trust is not about knowing; it's about going. When God whispers to you what to do, He's already made room for your yes.

Questions for Reflection:
- Where in your life are you waiting for permission to obey?
- Whose approval are you afraid of losing?

- What would you do if you weren't afraid of what others think?
- How does your obedience make room for others to obey?
- What keeps you from fully trusting the invitation to act?

Action Steps:

- Write down one area where you feel God calling you to obey.
- Identify the fears or people holding you back.
- Take one small step of obedience this week—no explanations, just faith.
- Write "I have permission" across a blank page. Beneath it, list three things God has already called you to do. Circle the one you've delayed. Take one step this week toward completing it.

Prayer:

"Lord, give me the boldness to obey You even when it's unpopular. Let my loyalty be to You above all else. Lord, I release my need for more signs. Let Your whisper be enough. Where You have spoken, give me the courage to obey without delay. Make my yes swift, sacred, and surrendered."

7

The Assignment That Found You

The assignment that found you speaks to the moments you didn't chase but that you were chosen for.

This chapter invites you to

- reflect on moments when purpose pursued you before you felt prepared.
- explore biblical examples like Moses, Jonah, and Gideon.
- practice identifying divine assignments that arrived unexpectedly.
- surrender the belief that readiness is a prerequisite for calling.
- declare trust in God's equipping for what He's already assigned.

Esther 4:14 declares, "For if you remain silent at this time, relief and deliverance for the Jews will arise from another place. … And who knows but that you have come to your royal position for such a time as this?" (NIV). This verse speaks to the mystery of divine timing, when purpose arrives not through planning but through providence. Esther didn't seek her moment; it found her. Her story reminds us that divine assignments often come disguised as interruptions, urgencies, or impossible choices. They don't wait for our readiness; they summon our obedience.

Sometimes purpose doesn't knock; it interrupts. Moses was tending sheep in Midian, far from the palace and even farther from confidence, when a burning bush turned an ordinary day into a divine summons (Exodus 3). Jonah tried to outrun his assignment, boarding a ship in the opposite direction, but purpose pursued him into the depths until he surrendered (Jonah 1–2). Gideon was hiding in fear, threshing wheat in secret, when an angel called him "mighty warrior"—a title that felt laughable in the moment but that later proved prophetic (Judges 6). Each of them was found by an assignment they didn't seek, didn't feel ready for, and didn't fully understand. But God doesn't wait for our readiness— He meets us in our reluctance. The assignment that finds you often reveals the strength you didn't know you had and the God who never stopped seeing it.

> *God doesn't wait for our readiness—He meets us in our reluctance.*

There is a quiet mystery in the way purpose pursues us. Unlike goals we chase, assignments often arrive unannounced, wrapped in discomfort, obscured by transition, and anchored in divine timing. We don't always choose them. Sometimes, they choose us. And when they do, it feels less like ambition and more like submission, less like strategy and more like surrender. No matter who you are or what you

> *There is a quiet mystery in the way purpose pursues us.*

do, you may have noticed that the most sacred roles you've walked into weren't part of a five-year plan; they were hidden in life's interruptions. The assignment that found you is the one that didn't ask for a résumé, permission, or confidence; it simply asked for your yes.

One afternoon, while volunteering at a charitable health clinic as a family nurse practitioner, I was asked by one of the medical providers if I would consider teaching at one of the local colleges. Mind you, I was not looking into a teaching career, but I obeyed the divine tap on the shoulder and completed the application for an adjunct professor the next day. This began my journey into the world of academia.

> *The assignment that found you is the one that didn't ask for a résumé, permission, or confidence; it simply asked for your yes.*

I wasn't looking for this assignment. I was managing my life, trying to stay faithful, trying to hide from the spotlight. But there it was: my name on something eternal. It didn't come from striving or ambition, but from sovereign appointment and availability. Maybe you operate in a high-stakes, high-output environment. Divine whispers will anchor you in identity and intimacy. They will remind you that even your purpose must be stewarded in surrender.

Divine ambush is the holy disruption that overtakes our carefully laid plans. Like Moses at the burning bush or Mary receiving the angel's announcement, these moments are

> *Divine ambush is the holy disruption that overtakes our carefully laid plans.*

invitations not to comfort, but to courage. A divine ambush is when God's purpose collides with our present and we realize we are standing in a story far larger than ourselves. It's not about being prepared; it's about being positioned.

Divine Interruption

Biblically, divine assignments are often disguised as detours. Ruth found hers in a barley field, following grief. Mary heard hers from an angel in the quiet of Nazareth. Saul met his on the road to Damascus, with no warning or negotiation.

In each case, the assignment was uninvited, yet unmistakable:

- Ruth was gleaning scraps.
- Mary was engaged to be married.
- Saul was en route to persecute.

These stories tell us something critical: Assignments don't always come through elevation. Instead, they often arrive through interruption. They find us in the valley or by quiet streams of water instead of the mountaintop. And when they do, they disrupt our destiny.

Divine interruptions are often God's gentle way of realigning our steps with His purposes. They may come when we're overcommitted, serving as a sacred redirection to restore clarity. Sometimes they arrive as unexpected burdens or nudges, calling

> *Divine interruptions are often God's gentle way of realigning our steps with His purposes.*

us to intercede in situations we hadn't even noticed. These

interruptions can also serve as quiet confirmations, affirming decisions that others may question but that are deeply rooted in obedience. And perhaps most tenderly, they reveal where growth is needed, where grace must be extended, or where a holy pause invites us to rest and recalibrate. What feels like disruption may actually be divine choreography. Whispers are also the fuel for prophetic writing; they are what birth books like this one. Not slogans or trends, but the quiet pulse of heaven translated to the page.

Timeline of Divine Intersections

To reflect on these moments, consider creating a timeline of divine intersections. This is a spiritual exercise in remembrance: tracing the unexpected turns, the conversations that shifted your direction, the invitations that felt premature but proved providential. These are the places where heaven interrupted your hesitation and purpose emerged from what once felt like a detour. Sometimes, you don't go looking for your calling—your calling finds you. It shows up in a conversation, a crisis, or a moment of clarity. It interrupts your plans, challenges your comfort, and demands your attention. This chapter is about those divine assignments that seem to find you when you least expect them and how to respond when they do. Many of the most powerful assignments in Scripture and in life weren't planned; they were discovered.

Modern examples of such assignments include

- a teacher who becomes a counselor after helping a student through trauma;

- a businessperson who starts a nonprofit after witnessing injustice; and
- a drug addict who becomes a preacher after attaining spiritual freedom.

Assignment before readiness invites you to name the moments when your calling came. Perhaps you were thrust into leadership (like I was at the age of twelve), asked to speak, write, mentor, or serve before you felt qualified. What did that experience reveal about God's timing, your identity, and the way grace equips us in motion? These reflections become sacred markers, evidence that readiness is not a prerequisite for obedience and that divine ambushes are often the birthplace of legacy. It's not always an angelic announcement or a divine dream. Often, it's a quiet conviction, a weight in your spirit that won't lift, a nudge to act, speak, write, serve, or stand when you'd prefer to be silent or still.

Here are some examples of signs to look for:

- A sacred burden you can't ignore
- A door you never planned to walk through that feels divinely unlocked
- A skill set suddenly activated in a moment of need
- A role that stretches your faith while affirming your grace

For me, these signs look like the student who suddenly asks for prayer or the writing prompt that speaks louder than my calendar. These aren't coincidences. They're clues. Assignments don't cater to convenience; they draw you into covenant. This reminds us that when

> **Assignments don't cater to convenience; they draw you into covenant.**

God gives us an assignment, it's rarely about what's easy. It's about what's eternal.

Divine assignments often interrupt your plans, stretch your faith, require sacrifice, and demand obedience, even when it's uncomfortable. But in doing so, they pull you deeper into relationship with God. They're not transactional; they're transformational. You're not just completing a task; you're entering a covenant of trust, surrender, and partnership with the One who called you.

The Difference Between Role and Assignment

In professional and ministry life, it's easy to confuse roles with assignments. Roles are structured: They come with titles, job descriptions, and expectations. Assignments, however, carry divine weight. They might overlap with your role, but they are deeper than that.

- A **role** may be teaching a class. An **assignment** could be mentoring a struggling student through personal loss using spiritual insight and healing presence.
- A **role** may be presenting at a workshop. An **assignment** could be using that moment to plant seeds of courage in someone battling a stronghold.
- A **role** may be writing a curriculum. An **assignment** could be embedding spiritual truth into a discussion.

Roles are visible. Assignments are often hidden in how we carry those roles. Recognizing an assignment means being spiritually alert in all settings. It means realizing that the true ministry may be happening beneath the surface of task and title.

Let's look at biblical figures who embodied assignments that found them:

- **Nehemiah** was a cupbearer, not a prophet, priest, or warrior. Yet, the burden of the broken walls of Jerusalem stirred him. That burden became his divine assignment. It wasn't his job; it was his calling.
- **Deborah** was a judge by role, but a warrior, prophet, and deliverer by assignment. Her obedience to speak and lead brought Israel into victory.
- **Samuel** was a young boy ministering in the temple. One night, the voice of God called him—not through Eli or through ritual, but directly. His lifelong prophetic assignment began with a whisper in the dark.

These stories affirm that divine assignments don't wait until we're ready. They call us into readiness through obedience. When divine assignment disrupts comfort, it rarely does so gently. It stretches our sense of identity, interrupts well-laid plans, and often challenges our credibility. Consider Moses, who wrestled with a speech impediment; Jeremiah, who felt too young; Esther, who risked her life; and Paul, whose past was marked by persecution. Each of them faced the tension between inadequacy and calling, and yet, their obedience became the bridge to impact. My assignment as a mentor and minister of the gospel came at a time when I was busy with work and rearing young children. I did not feel ready or qualified, but the assignment was ready for me.

If you feel unqualified when your assignment finds you, you're in good company. Scripture is full of reluctant leaders and hesitant prophets. Sometimes, like Jonah, we run. Sometimes, like Peter, we deny. But the assignment doesn't vanish; it only waits—not with impatience, but with faithfulness. And when we're ready to turn toward it, grace stands ready to meet us, arms wide with welcome and strength for the journey.

Writing as an Assignment

The assignment to write this book began as a sentence: "You were made for this." It was a phrase that refused to leave my spirit. I didn't choose it; it chose me. *The Whisper of Purpose* wasn't a branding idea; it was a divine whisper.

> *If you feel unqualified when your assignment finds you, you're in good company.*

The chapters, reflections, and tools in this book are not just content; they're the products of my obedience. Assignments are written not for popularity, but for legacy. Legacy doesn't begin with audience; it begins with surrender. How do you know when something is more than a coincidence? When is it a calling? These were the questions I wrestled with in this season of writing.

Confirmation plays a vital role in discerning whether an assignment is truly from God. It may show up as repeated themes in prayer, Scripture, or conversations, threads that seem to weave themselves into your awareness. You might experience an inner peace that defies outer uncertainty, a quiet assurance that steadies you even when circumstances don't. And often, trusted voices will affirm what you're sensing, offering encouragement and clarity that will help you move forward with confidence. Divine assignments rarely come without risk, but they always come with grace. (Note: *The Assignment: Discovering and Living in Your Purpose* by Kim Brooks offers a practical and faith-filled guide to navigating life's transitions with intentionality.)

God Often Speaks Through Patterns, Not Pressure

When purpose finds you, your first response might not be excitement, but fear, doubt, reluctance, or resistance. Unexpected assignments often stir up a chorus of internal resistance. Thoughts like "I'm not qualified," "This isn't part of my plan," or "What if I fail?" echo the very human tension between comfort and calling.

These reactions aren't new—in fact, they're woven throughout Scripture in the stories of those who were called beyond their perceived limits. Jonah ran from Nineveh, resisting the assignment with outright defiance. Jeremiah protested, claiming he was too young to speak on God's behalf. Gideon, overwhelmed by insecurity, declared, "I'm the least in my family." Each of these biblical figures voiced doubts that mirror our own. Yet, their stories remind us that divine assignments are rarely about our qualifications; they're about God's empowerment. Resistance may be part of the journey, but it doesn't have to be the end. Obedience, even when reluctant, opens the door to transformation.

At some point, the running must give way to trusting. Surrender becomes the sacred bridge between calling and impact, built not on certainty but on faith. Your yes matters more than your readiness, because you don't need to

> **Surrender becomes the sacred bridge between calling and impact.**

have all the answers; obedience is about yielding to the One who does. Surrender looks like releasing your timeline, loosening your grip on control, and saying yes before the full picture is revealed. It's trusting God more than your own understanding and choosing to walk in the assignment even when the path feels unclear. Rather than passive, this kind of surrender is a courageous act of alignment.

Obedience will cost something: sacrifice, discomfort, or change. But it also brings a depth of fulfillment that comfort could never offer. It aligns your life with divine purpose, and in that alignment, you find peace, clarity, and the joy of walking in step with God's heart.

The Whisper of Alignment

When an assignment finds you, it's not random. It's aligned. It fits your gifts. It speaks to your experiences. It requires your sensitivity. It honors your testimony. You may feel unprepared, but you are not unequipped. Isaiah 61 speaks of divine reversal: beauty for ashes, joy for mourning, praise for heaviness. This is what my assignments did: They redeemed what was broken and repurposed it for glory. You were found, even if you weren't really lost, because you were ready.

You don't need to chase assignment; it's something you receive. Once you say yes, the journey begins. It's rarely easy, but it's always worth it. Once you've said yes, you must stay rooted in prayer and Scripture, surround yourself with wise counsel, keep showing up (even when it's hard), regularly check in with God, be open to course corrections, and remember why you started.

A whisper-ready posture is the soil where calling takes root and grows. If you're wondering whether you're called, you're already listening—and that is the first act of obedience.

Here are five actions you can take to help your assignment find you:

1. **Pray for clarity**. Ask God to reveal the nature and scope of the assignment. What's the "why" beneath the "what"?
2. **Move past insecurity**. Assignments rarely land on qualified grounds. They grow in the soil of willingness.
3. **Document the journey**. Journal. Reflect. Write. Your assignment is for you now, but it's also a blueprint for others later.
4. **Honor the people along the path**. Your family, friends, colleagues, neighbors, community, and church family aren't background characters. They are divine companions in your assignment journey.
5. **Guard against comparison**. Your assignment is tailored. Don't dilute it by measuring it against someone else's calling.

Reflection and Application

Illustration: Your assignment is like a wave that reaches the shore without warning. You didn't summon it. You won't see it coming. But it will arrive with force and purpose, reshaping the landscape of your life. Divine assignments are sent from beyond your horizon and are always perfectly timed.

Scripture Focus: *"You did not choose Me, but I chose you and appointed you…"* (John 15:16, NIV)

Devotional Thought: Not every purpose is planned; some are planted. God's assignments often arrive in disguise: a sudden need, a whispered invitation, a burden you didn't ask for but can't ignore. Convenience didn't factor into your recruitment; you were positioned by grace. When divine assignments find you, they stir both holy hesitation and sacred boldness. Like Moses, you may ask, "Why me?" But the assignment has already answered that question: *Because you're His.*

Questions for Reflection:

- What assignment found you before you were ready?
- Has something been repeatedly showing up in your life that feels like more than coincidence?
- What assignment might God be inviting you into right now?
- What fears or excuses have been holding you back?
- What assignment has found you unexpectedly?
- How has obedience opened doors you never knocked on?
- Where do you feel divine positioning in your current season?

Action Steps:

- Write down any recurring burdens, themes, or opportunities you've noticed.
- Share your sense of calling with a trusted friend or mentor.

- Take one step—however small—toward saying yes to an assignment.
- Write down one area of your life you didn't plan but now feel deeply purposed in. Share it with someone who may be resisting a similar call.

Prayer:

"Lord, Help me to accept the assignment that found me with holy confidence. Even when it's unannounced, inconvenient, or beyond my understanding, let my heart recognize Your hand in it. I receive the assignment with faith, knowing You walk with me every step of the way. Amen."

8

When Doors Close Softly

The image of doors closing softly doesn't refer to slammed exits but to sacred transitions.

This chapter invites you to

- reflect on moments when opportunities ended without explanation or closure.
- explore biblical examples like Paul's blocked journey, Naomi's return to Bethlehem, and the rich young ruler's quiet departure.
- practice identifying the spiritual significance of gentle endings.
- surrender the need to force open what God has gently shut.
- declare peace in transition and trust in divine redirection.

Revelation 3:7 offers a profound assurance: "What He opens no one can shut, and what He shuts no one can open" (NIV). This verse reframes closed doors as redirection. In a culture that often equates opportunity with favor, it's easy to see a shut door as a failure. But Scripture reminds us that divine sovereignty governs both the openings and the closings.

Some doors don't slam shut; they close softly, leaving behind questions, quiet grief, and the ache of redirection. Paul experienced this on his missionary journey when the Holy Spirit blocked his path to Asia (Acts 16:6–7). What might have seemed like rejection was in fact redirection: the Holy Spirit was guiding him toward Macedonia and a greater assignment. Naomi returned to Bethlehem with empty hands and a heavy heart, the door to her former life quietly closed by loss. Yet in that return, God was already preparing a new beginning through Ruth. The rich young ruler, after hearing Jesus' invitation to surrender everything, walked away in sorrow (Mark 10:22). The door to deeper purpose stood open, but he couldn't step through it. These stories remind us that when doors close softly, it's not always failure; it's often formation. God speaks in the hush, leads through the pause, and waits patiently at the threshold of our next yes.

When God closes a door, it may feel like a punishment in the moment, but it is often to protect us and guide us toward something more aligned with His purpose. When God closed the door on medical school, I was hurt and disappointed, but His redirection was purposeful. These are the closures we often miss in the moment, as their silence is mistaken for coincidence or delay. But spiritually, the soft close is often the kindest form of divine redirection. It beckons us to pause, reflect, and trust that silence itself might be a signal.

In life and calling, the soft closure is a message from God. It's the job interview you were never called back after, the ministry initiative that fizzled, the friendship that faded without conflict, the book proposal

> *In life and calling, the soft closure is a message from God.*

that was quietly turned down, a dream that slowly lost its spark. These soft closures can be confusing and painful, especially when we believed they were part of our purpose.

But what if they're redirections instead of rejections? The opportunity seemed aligned, yet it quietly disappeared. These moments speak in hushed tones: *Not this. Not now. Not anymore.* In spiritual maturity, we learn to honor the whisper—which is harder than honoring the shout. At least when things explode, you know they're over. But when doors close softly, they can leave you wondering if you misheard God, missed your chance, or misunderstood the season. God's gentle no is often preservation. The key is interpreting divine redirection without resentment.

> *God's gentle no is often preservation.*

The Kindness of Quiet Closures

A door closing softly reflects the gentleness of God's character. He does not yank us violently from pathways that no longer serve His plan. Rather, He redirects with compassion. As Psalm 23:2 reminds us, "He leads me beside the still waters" (NKJV). That's a leadership model of peace and patience. Closed doors aren't a punishment or failure, but protection dressed in humility. They're divine nos spoken with grace. Consider Acts 16:6, when Paul was, "kept by the Holy Spirit from preaching the word in the province of Asia" (NIV). It wasn't a dramatic restraint, but a quiet one. That restraint led him to Macedonia, where an entirely new sphere of ministry awaited. Closed doors are not dead ends but rerouted roads.

One of the first signs of a closing door is a subtle lack of peace where peace once lived. What was once a place of clarity and comfort begins to feel unsettled, like a quiet dissonance. The path ahead may grow dim. It's as if the light that once guided your steps has been gently withdrawn, leaving you to pause and consider whether that journey is meant to continue.

You may also feel a spiritual nudge to move on, even in the absence of external confirmation. No one else may see or affirm it, but deep within, you sense the invitation to release and realign. And perhaps most telling of all is the quiet withdrawal of grace for a particular endeavor. What once flowed easily now feels strained. The oil that once anointed your efforts seems to have been washed away—likely in preparation for something new. These moments ask for reflection instead of resistance.

The Holy Spirit may not thunder through your calendar, but He'll whisper through your discomfort. The grace lifts. The momentum fades. You begin sensing the shift in discernment. You don't always get a burning bush. Sometimes, you just get a holy hush. You may recall seasons when things felt divinely aligned, and yet, they dissolved without chaos. These are soft closures, and they deserve reverence. They teach us that obedience is not just about staying; it's also about knowing when to leave. Purpose is discovered as much in discerning as in doing. There are seasons when the boldest act of faith is quietly exiting something God is no longer in. This release makes room for the next assignment to unfold.

The Pain of Closed Doors

Closed doors hurt, especially when we've invested time, energy, and hope into those endeavors. While they can feel like failure or punishment, these closed doors are often protection. It's okay to mourn the door that closed. Closed doors sting because they challenge our expectations, confront our sense of control, and force us to grieve what could have been. We may experience disappointment, confusion, or even anger at God, and we feel a temptation to question our worth or calling. *Letting Go: The Pathway of Surrender* by David R. Hawkins affirms that when doors close—especially softly—it may be an invitation to release control and trust divine timing.

> *Closed doors hurt, especially when we've invested time, energy, and hope into those endeavors.*

Let's consider some more biblical examples of redirection:

- **Elijah's Cave** (1 Kings 19): Elijah expected God in the earthquake and the fire, but God spoke in a still small voice. Elijah's assignment was being recalibrated through sacred silence.
- **Jesus in Nazareth** (Mark 6): Jesus returned to His hometown, but He could not perform many miracles there due to unbelief. He left quietly. There was no drama, only a soft shift of focus to other regions.
- **David and the Temple** (1 Chronicles 22): David had the heart to build the temple, but the assignment was not his. God told him gently, "You will not build my house." This wasn't a rejection; it was a realignment. David honored it by preparing Solomon's way.

These stories remind us that obedience sometimes looks like walking away quietly when grace has exited the room. God doesn't always shout His no. Sometimes, He simply lets something fade. He allows a door to close softly because He's guiding us with kindness. Divine redirection is often subtle. You feel a lack of peace, experience a series of delays, and sense a quiet inner knowing that it's time to move on.

Jesus didn't heal in every town or respond to every request. In John 5:19, He says, "the Son can do nothing by Himself; He can do only what He sees His Father doing" (NIV). His restraint was rooted in perfect discernment. In Mark 1:38, Jesus even leaves a town where people are still seeking Him: "Let us go somewhere else—to the nearby villages—so I can preach there also. That is why I have come" (NIV).

In spiritual discernment, the ability to recognize when grace has lifted is paramount. When a door closes, we have a choice: cling to what was or trust what's next. Letting go is an act of faith. Obedience doesn't always end in triumph; it sometimes ends in release.

> **When a door closes, we have a choice: cling to what was or trust what's next.**

Let go of the script you thought God would follow. Trust that His vision stretches beyond your horizon. Like Abraham leaving without knowing the destination, surrender is not weakness; it's worship.

Release is the only way forward. Joseph forgave his brothers not because they deserved it, but because he refused to be defined by betrayal. Loss is real, so feel it, name it, and honor it, but don't let it write your future. Even Jesus wept at Lazarus' tomb. Grief is part of faith, but resurrection always follows surrender.

Gratitude for Closed Doors

Practicing gratitude for closed doors is a spiritual discipline that transforms our perspective. It invites us to look back and name the closed doors that once felt disappointing but that now reveal unexpected peace. This might include journaling about specific moments when a no led to a deeper yes or writing prayers of thanksgiving for the clarity that came through loss. Gratitude doesn't need to erase the ache to honor the wisdom of God's timing.

So, how do we steward the doors that close softly?

1. **Honor the exit**. Don't belittle what once was. Speak of it with gratitude, even when you don't fully understand the ending.
2. **Avoid forcing reentry**. If grace has lifted, it's wise not to pry the door open. Forced reentry into a closed space can breed frustration or spiritual dullness.
3. **Listen for the next invitation**. Closed doors often precede open ones. But they also sharpen our listening. Ask, "Where is grace now? What is the Spirit emphasizing now?"
4. **Record the transition**. In your journal or devotional mapping guide, document what has closed. That act of recognition will honor the shift and allow for reflection later.
5. **Speak life**, **not loss**. Don't define the closed door as failure. Speak of it as redirection. That reframing can strengthen others who silently struggle.

Where are you right now in your journey? Pause and consider what doors may be closing and how you can best respond in gratitude. As you reflect, remember that closed doors are not signs of failure; they are sacred signals of redirection. Sometimes, God's mercy is disguised as a gentle ending, guiding you away from what no longer serves your growth and toward what aligns with His greater plan. Gratitude in these moments is a declaration of trust. So breathe deeply, release what's behind you, and step forward with faith, knowing that every closed door makes room for something divinely appointed to open.

The Power in Gentle Endings

There's a sacred authority in closing things softly. You may retire from a ministry role without bitterness. You may shift careers without declaring it on social media. You may leave a season quietly, knowing obedience matters more than optics.

Soft closures teach others to trust timing and walk in quiet courage. In Isaiah 30:21, it says, "Your ears will hear a voice behind you, saying, 'This is the way; walk in it'" (NIV). Notice the voice comes *after* the decision. That's permission to trust your spiritual instinct. What closed door brought unexpected peace in your life? Perhaps it was a missed opportunity that preserved your energy, a relationship that ended before it could wound deeper, or a dream that was deferred to make room for something more eternal. These reflections become testimonies of trust, evidence that peace often follows obedience, even when the path is unclear. Every closed door carries a lesson. If we're willing to reflect, we'll find wisdom in the disappointment. Sometimes the lesson is simply "Wait."

Maturing Through Closed Doors

Growth doesn't come simply from moving on; it comes from reflecting, pausing long enough to process what God is teaching in the midst of transition. Maturity is forged in the quiet spaces of journaling, prayer, and wise counsel, where deeper meaning begins to surface and shape us.

When one door closes, it's easy to fixate on what's behind us. But God never closes a door without preparing another to open. The challenge is to stop staring at the old one long enough to perceive the new one. Signs of a new direction often include a renewed sense of passion or vision, unexpected opportunities that feel divinely timed, and a deep sense of peace and alignment that confirms you're on the right path.

To stay open and expectant, keep your heart soft and your spirit attentive. Don't rush the process. Clarity often comes slowly, like dawn breaking over the horizon. Isaiah 43:19 offers a timely reminder: "See, I am doing a new thing … do you not perceive it?" (NIV). The new thing is already unfolding. The invitation is to notice. Mentoring others through soft closures requires sensitivity. Avoid fixing what God has gently ended. Don't rush to reopen their doors. Sit with them. Reflect with them.

> *Avoid fixing what God has gently ended.*

You don't need fireworks to finish a page, just a final sentence that settles your spirit. Honor the whisper, then ask, "What is the next word Heaven wants to write?" When doors close softly, it's easy to misinterpret the moment. But in God's economy, a gentle closing is often a gracious redirection. What feels like failure may actually be formation, shaping your character and refining your calling. Confusion isn't always a lack of clarity; sometimes it's divine calibration, aligning your heart with heaven's rhythm. And silence is not absence; it's strategy. God is still speaking, even when the volume is low.

Reflection and Application

Illustration: Whether quietly or loudly, a door that closes still changes your direction. Sometimes God's no is whispered, not shouted.

Scripture Focus: *"I have placed before you an open door that no one can shut."* (Revelation 3:8, NIV)

Devotional Thought: Some doors close for your protection. You were headed somewhere that looked good, but God saw deeper. The soft close may feel like loss, but it's a provision. In discernment, we recognize that blocked paths are actually pauses for rerouting, refuge, and refinement. Honor the shut door. It may be God's way of ensuring your feet don't outrun His favor.

Questions for Reflection:

- What door in your life has recently closed, softly or suddenly?
- What recently closed door do you still question?
- How have you responded to that closure: with resistance, resentment, or release?
- What did that closed door preserve in you?
- What closed door brought you unexpected peace?
- Where might God be redirecting you through gentle endings?

Action Steps:

- Write a thank-you note to a closed door. Name what you gained from its absence. Reflect on how peace often follows release.
- Ask God to show you where He's leading you next.
- Practice gratitude for what the closed door taught you.

Prayer: "Lord, help me not chase what You've lovingly closed. Teach me to trust the silence of sealed pathways. Show me the grace hidden in goodbyes."

9

Faithfulness In The Fog

Faithfulness in the fog means walking with holy courage when visibility fades and clarity hides.

This chapter invites you to

- reflect on seasons when clarity was absent but commitment was required.
- explore biblical examples like Joseph in prison, the Israelites in the wilderness, and Habakkuk's lament.
- practice naming areas where you've remained faithful despite uncertainty.
- surrender the need for full visibility before taking the next step.
- declare trust in God's presence even when the path is unclear.

Hebrews 11:1 declares, "Now faith is confidence in what we hope for and assurance about what we do not see" (NIV). This verse invites us into the paradox of faith, where certainty is not required and clarity is not the goal. Faith is not the absence of doubt; it is trust in the midst of that doubt. It is the ability to walk forward when the path is obscured, to hope when outcomes are unknown, and to remain anchored when visibility is low.

Faithfulness in the fog is choosing trust when clarity is withheld. Joseph sat in prison, falsely accused and forgotten. Yet he remained faithful, stewarding his gifts, interpreting dreams, and believing that God's favor hadn't left him. The Israelites wandered in the wilderness, surrounded by uncertainty and unmet expectations, yet God provided manna, water, and guidance by cloud and fire—a daily invitation to trust without a map. Habakkuk stood in lament, watching injustice rise and prayers go seemingly unanswered, yet he wrestled honestly with God and declared, "Though the fig tree does not bud…yet I will rejoice in the Lord" (Habakkuk 3:17–18, NIV). Each story reminds us that faith isn't proven in the light but forged in the fog. These figures teach us that fog doesn't impede God; it prepares us to encounter Him differently. When the path is unclear and the promise feels distant, faithfulness becomes the loudest declaration that God is still worthy.

Fog is not absence. It is presence obscured. It is light diffused through uncertainty, truth hidden in softness, and direction veiled but not denied. In spiritual life, the foggy seasons are the least welcomed but most formative. These are the days of hazy decision-making, indistinct outcomes, and questions answered only by silence. And yet, faithfulness in the fog is perhaps the most potent obedience of all. To walk when you cannot see is to declare that you trust the One who sees all. Fog isn't meant to

> **Fog is not absence. It is presence obscured.**

disorient but to discipline. It quiets. It forces the soul to listen beneath noise, to choose depth over speed and trust over trajectory. When God allows fog, He is not forsaking clarity; He is forming character and building our faith.

Clarity is not a prerequisite for movement. Faith is defined not by certainty, but by assurance in uncertainty. It's why the psalmist declares, "Your word is a lamp for my feet" (Psalm 119:105, NIV).

> *Clarity is not a prerequisite for movement.*

Lamps illuminate inches, not miles. Faithfulness in the fog requires walking by lamplight, step by surrendered step. There are seasons when God gives you a vision and seasons when He simply gives you instructions. There are times when the way ahead sparkles with confirmation, and there are times when fog rolls in so thick, you're not even sure if you're still moving in the right direction. Many seasons of ministry in my life have required walking in the fog and trusting God for the next step.

Fog Is Sacred Uncertainty

Fog doesn't erase the road; it simply limits how far ahead we can see. In spiritual terms, fog is the space where God invites us to slow down, to listen more closely, and to trust more deeply. Sacred uncertainty is the place where faith is formed. In her book *Anonymous: Jesus' Hidden Years...and Yours,* Alicia Britt Chole affirms that unseen faithfulness is often the soil of deep transformation. The fog demands a different kind of faithfulness: not dramatic leaps,

> *Fog is the space where God invites us to slow down, to listen more closely, and to trust more deeply.*

but deliberate footsteps. It's showing up for class with lessons still unclear. Writing the pages that haven't yet formed their message. Praying prayers that feel unanswered but still essential. This is fidelity to the process, not just to the product.

Consider the Israelites gathering manna. All they had was daily bread. Faithfulness meant trusting in the provision and gathering it. It was cyclical, humble, and sacred. Likewise, in my work and ministry life, foggy seasons required rhythmic obedience, such as leading when the outcomes felt invisible, trusting repeatedly in the face of failures, and doing the next right thing, even when the "why" was unclear.

There are seasons in life when the future feels blurry. You know you're called, you know you're loved, but you don't know what's next. The fog of uncertainty can be disorienting. You can't see the full picture, and every step feels risky, but you need to keep forging ahead.

Fog as a Ministry Filter

In ministry, fog has a strange way of revealing motives. When the applause fades, when certainty evaporates, what remains?

- **Are we still faithful when no one notices?** True obedience is forged in obscurity. Like Elijah in the wilderness, God often does His deepest work in hidden places.
- **Do we still serve when progress stalls?** Ministry isn't a sprint; it's a pilgrimage. When growth feels stagnant, faithfulness becomes the fruit. I have been tempted to quit several times, but then I remembered that the journey doesn't end here.

- **Will we still encourage others when our own path is shrouded?** Encouragement in the fog is a prophetic act. It says, "I believe in light, even when it's dark."

Jesus modeled this in His hidden years: decades of obscurity before public ministry. He was faithful in silence. For leaders, the fog reveals the foundation. When visibility disappears, vision must rise.

Writing in the Fog

As I wrote *The Whisper of Purpose*, I encountered fog: chapters that resisted completion, ideas that began strong but refused resolution, a holy frustration that came from knowing something is there but not yet available. Writing through the sacred fog was holy work. The fog taught me spiritual endurance. And every sentence formed in it became an altar, a declaration that I would trust the whisper even when the words weren't clear.

Legacy doesn't begin with a polished plan; it begins with a courageous yes.

- **Writing by faith, not inspiration:** Sometimes the pen moves before the heart catches up. Faithful writing trusts that meaning will emerge in time.
- **Creating chapters before knowing where they'll fit:** Like Noah building the ark before the rain came, obedience often precedes understanding. Each chapter is a plank in the vessel of purpose.
- **Editing a paragraph you suspect has a purpose that hasn't yet been discerned:** The Spirit often whispers through fragments. What feels unfinished may be the seed of someone else's breakthrough.

This is where legacy thrives: in courage, in quiet persistence, in trusting the Author.

The Mentor's Role in the Fog

Faithfulness during foggy seasons requires spiritual companionship. When I think of the steadfast love, wisdom, encouragement, and intercession from my church family, spiritual mentors, and close friends, I realize they were never background characters; they've been my fog-guides. Mentors in fog don't give answers, but they do hold space. They remind you of past clarity, affirm your endurance, intercede when your voice falters, and celebrate your stillness. When fog descends, their voices become steady, guiding echoes.

Biblical Examples of Mentorship in the Fog

1. Moses and Joshua

- **Fog**: Joshua faced the daunting task of leading Israel after Moses' death.
- **Mentor's Role**: Moses prepared Joshua gradually, bringing him into sacred spaces (Exodus 24:13), entrusting him with leadership tasks (Exodus 17:9), and affirming his calling publicly (Deuteronomy 31:7).
- **Impact**: Joshua stepped into leadership with courage, despite the path being unclear, because his mentorship was faithful.

2. Elijah and Elisha

- **Fog**: Elisha was called suddenly while plowing fields; his future was unclear.
- **Mentor's Role**: Elijah invited Elisha into prophetic ministry, modeled spiritual authority, and passed on a double portion of his spirit (2 Kings 2:9–14).
- **Impact**: Elisha's boldness in ministry was forged through proximity to Elijah's faith during uncertain times.

3. Paul and Timothy

- **Fog**: Timothy was young and timid, and he faced opposition in ministry.
- **Mentor's Role**: Paul wrote letters of encouragement (1 Timothy and 2 Timothy), affirmed Timothy's gifts, and gave practical guidance for leadership amid persecution.
- **Impact**: Timothy became a trusted leader because Paul walked with him through the fog.

4. Naomi and Ruth

- **Fog**: Ruth was a Moabite widow in a foreign land, uncertain of her future.
- **Mentor's Role**: Naomi guided Ruth with wisdom, cultural insight, and spiritual discernment—especially in navigating Boaz's field and redemption (Ruth 3).
- **Impact**: Ruth's obedience and Naomi's mentorship led to divine alignment and legacy.

5. Samuel and David

- **Fog**: David was anointed as king while still a shepherd, with no roadmap to royalty.
- **Mentor's Role**: Samuel anointed David, affirmed his calling, and served as a spiritual anchor during Saul's reign.
- **Impact**: David's confidence in God's timing was shaped by Samuel's prophetic mentorship.

The Nature of Uncertainty

Uncertainty is woven into the fabric of human experience. For people of faith, however, it's not merely a challenge to endure; it's a sacred terrain to walk across with God. What makes uncertainty so uncomfortable is our longing for control and predictability. We want to know what's next, to map the journey before we take the first step. Beneath that desire lies a fear of missteps, choosing wrongly, or veering off course. We often equate clarity with sovereignty, assuming that if the path is well lit, it must be God-ordained.

> *We want to know what's next, to map the journey before we take the first step.*

Yet Scripture reveals a different rhythm, one in which God often leads through mystery. Abraham, called by God, left everything familiar without knowing his destination. Instead of following sight, he followed trust (Hebrews 11:8, NIV). The Israelites, too, journeyed through the wilderness guided by a cloud by day

> *God is not just at the destination; He is in the journey itself.*

and fire by night. Their movement was moment by moment, step by step, dependent on divine presence rather than human planning.

Faith doesn't erase uncertainty; it redefines it. It invites us to walk with full surrender. In the absence of answers, we must lean into assurance. In the fog of the unknown, we listen for the whisper, and in every step, we discover that God is not just at the destination; He is in the journey itself.

Lessons in Foggy Decision-Making

If there's one area where fog is common, it's healthcare. I've seen many complex cases with unclear symptoms and inconclusive labs, and through all of these foggy situations, I have learned to use reason in uncertainty. I have had to

> *You can't see the full picture but you're still called to move in faith.*

be faithful to the process when the outcome was still uncertain. I have learned to say, "I don't have the final answer, but I'm walking with integrity until I do." That posture is the space between revelation and fulfillment, where you can't see the full picture but you're still called to move in faith.

When clarity is absent, your posture can become a prophetic declaration:

- Kneeling says, "I trust You even when I don't understand."
- Standing firm says, "I believe Your promise even when I can't see it."
- Hands lifted say, "I surrender the outcome to You."

In other words, your posture *prophecies* your faith. It declares what you believe about God's character, even when the path is unclear. It may seem reactive, but it's revelatory. Confusing as it may be in the moment, fog is divine restraint. It asks, "Will you obey without details? Will you trust the nudge, even when the narrative is unfinished?" This is where discernment is key: knowing not just what to do but when to wait, when to release, and when to rest. Discernment listens for nuance. It hears God saying, "Not now," rather than "Never."

Faith Over Sight

Faith is not a feeling; it's a decision to trust God even when you can't see the outcome. Hebrews 11:1 reminds us, "Now faith is confidence in what we hope for and assurance about what we do not see" (NIV). Walking by faith means

- trusting God's character more than your circumstances,
- believing His promises even when they feel distant, and
- moving forward without full visibility.

Remember: Faith is not blind. When the broader vision feels hazy and the future remains unformed, you only need to focus on the next right step. Obedience often begins in the quiet corners of our day: making the call, sending the email, showing up again and again. These small, seemingly mundane acts are the building blocks of trust and momentum. They are the daily yeses that shape a life of faithfulness.

Scripture reminds us that God provided only enough manna in the wilderness for each day at a time. The lesson was clear: Trust for today prepares the heart for tomorrow. There's grace in the portion, wisdom in the rhythm, and holiness in the ordinary. Faithfulness is cultivated in the mundane, in the unseen and uncelebrated moments when obedience whispers, "This is enough for now." In that whisper, we find the presence of God, steady and sure.

Action Steps in Ambiguity

God's presence brings peace and assurance that surpasses understanding (Philippians 4:7). Staying anchored requires you to trust God with the process when you can't see clearly and to lean on truths that hold you steady. Spiritual disciplines anchor us when the winds of uncertainty rise. Prayer and worship create space for communion, reminding us that we're not alone in the journey. Scripture meditation roots us in truth, offering clarity when emotions cloud our vision. And community, especially when paired with accountability, keeps us grounded, reminding us that the path of faith is never meant to be walked in isolation.

One of the most powerful ways to remain anchored is by remembering God's past faithfulness. Journaling answered prayers and reflecting on the ways He's led you before can rekindle trust when the future feels unclear. As Hebrews 6:19 reminds us, "We have this hope as an anchor for the soul" (NIV). It holds us fast, even if we can't see the outcome, because we trust the One who does.

Breath prayers can be a powerful practice in this space. These are short, rhythmic prayers whispered with each inhale and exhale, anchoring us in the present moment. In times of ambiguity, breath prayers like "[inhale] I trust… [exhale] …even now," or "[inhale] You are near… [exhale] I will not fear," help us remain grounded. They are gentle reminders that even in the fog, God is near.

What anchors you when your vision is blurred? What practices, Scriptures, or memories help you stay the course when certainty is unavailable? Perhaps it's the testimony of past faithfulness, the encouragement of community, or the quiet assurance that obedience doesn't require full understanding. These reflections are sacred markers, evidence that faith is forged in trust.

Reflection and Application

Illustration: Driving through fog requires trust in the road ahead. You may not be able to see far, but you must keep moving forward.

Scripture Focus: *"For we live by faith, not by sight."* (2 Corinthians 5:7, NIV)

Devotional Thought: Foggy seasons test your devotion, not your direction. When clarity withdraws and outcomes blur, faithfulness becomes the quiet rhythm of trust. In uncertainty, God's presence draws nearer, asking, "Will you follow the voice, even without a map?" Some of your greatest obedience will come in holy discomfort.

Questions for Reflection:

- How do you remain faithful when clarity is absent?
- What feels obscured but persistent?
- What has God previously spoken that still applies?

- How have you seen God's faithfulness in past seasons of uncertainty?
- Where in your life are you still showing up despite uncertainty?

Action Steps:

- Write down three truths about God's character that you can cling to in the fog.
- Create a "faithfulness journal" to track how God shows up in small ways.
- Reach out to a trusted friend or mentor for encouragement and prayer.
- Take one small step of obedience today.
- Light a candle during your devotional time this week. Let it illustrate how even a small flame—like daily obedience—pierces spiritual fog. Journal what the light reveals.

Prayer:

"Lord, when I cannot see, teach me to still respond. Let fog be my sanctuary. May my steps echo trust, even when the path grows dim. Lord, help me to remain faithful even when I can't see clearly. Let my trust in You be greater than my need for certainty. Amen."

10

Living Loudly From A Whisper

Living loudly from a whisper refers to the paradox of quiet callings becoming visible impact.

This chapter invites you to

- reflect on how quiet convictions have led to bold expressions of purpose.
- explore biblical examples like Jeremiah's fire in his bones, Mary Magdalene's testimony, and Peter's proclamation at Pentecost.
- practice identifying whispers that have shaped your public witness.
- surrender the fear of being misunderstood or dismissed.
- declare the courage to live out your calling with unapologetic faith.

Matthew 5:14 proclaims, "You are the light of the world. A city that is set on a hill cannot be hidden" (NKJV). This verse reminds us that our light is inherent. To follow Christ is to shine. Light doesn't strive; it simply reveals. In a world often cloaked in fear and silence, your voice, your story, and your obedience become radiant acts of courage.

Living loudly from a whisper means letting the quiet stirrings of God erupt into bold declaration. Jeremiah tried to stay silent, weary from rejection, but he confessed that God's word was like "a burning fire shut up in my bones"—too powerful to contain, too sacred to suppress (Jeremiah 20:9, NKJV). Mary Magdalene, once bound by seven demons, became the first witness of the resurrection, carrying the whispered truth of an empty tomb to trembling disciples. Her testimony wasn't polished; it was personal, and it changed history. Peter, who once denied Jesus in fear, stood at Pentecost with fire in his voice and the Spirit in his lungs, proclaiming the Gospel to thousands. Each of them began with a whisper—an encounter, a calling, a conviction—and chose to live it out loud. Their lives remind us that when God speaks softly, it's often the beginning of something that will shake the world.

Living loudly from a whisper also means you've decided that God's voice carries more weight than public opinion. It means you've stopped waiting for applause and started walking in assignment. Courage is what enables you to speak when silence feels safer, to act when delay feels easier, and to believe when doubt feels louder. That courage is often quiet, consistent, and deeply rooted in conviction. But make no mistake: It's holy.

> *Living loudly from a whisper means letting the quiet stirrings of God erupt into bold declaration.*

Throughout Scripture, we see courage paired with calling. Esther approached the king, in spite of her fear, because she was faithful. Peter stepped out of the boat onto the water because Jesus had called. Courage doesn't guarantee ease; it guarantees movement. And when you live loudly from a whisper, you declare to heaven and earth that God's voice is enough to guide your steps, shape your story, and fulfill your purpose.

The Power of a Whisper

It all started with a whisper. A quiet nudge. A still small voice. And yet, that whisper changed me. It changed everything. In the economy of heaven, *whispers* hold power. They summon prophets, reroute kings, birth assignments, and unearth purposes. What begins in stillness, if stewarded rightly, echoes boldly through generations.

The power of whisper says, "God spoke, and I responded." It is the decision to turn a sacred nudge into a public declaration, to take the quiet yes and embody it in a visible faith. It can shape classrooms, conversations, ministries, books, and prayers out of syllables God whispered in private.

> *The power of whisper says, "God spoke, and I responded."*

The Whisper: Divine Initiation

God's whispers are focused. Elijah experienced this firsthand (1 Kings 19). He expected God in wind, earthquake, and fire. But the Lord came in a *still small voice*. That whisper carried weight, direction, and comfort in a single breath.

God's voice is not found in the clamor of ambition or the spotlight of performance. It's discovered in the quiet corners where hearts

> *God's voice is not found in the clamor of ambition or the spotlight of performance.*

are postured to listen. He whispers to those in prayer closets long before they stand behind pulpits. He speaks in seasons of obscure preparation, where no one sees, before public elevation ever arrives. His revelations often come during long drives and in the stillness of journaling, before microphones and ministry teams enter the picture.

To live loudly from a whisper is to live from spiritual proximity and intimacy. God does not shout to compete with our distractions; He invites us closer. We must lean in, slow down, and surrender the need to be seen in order to truly hear. Revelation is reserved for those who dwell, not just visit.

Revelation—true, transformative insight from God—is not a casual encounter. It's not something stumbled upon in a moment of convenience or spiritual tourism. It's the fruit of dwelling. To dwell means to remain, abide, linger, and live in the presence of God. It's the posture of someone who doesn't just seek answers but also seeks relationship. Those who dwell are cultivating a life of communion.

In contrast, those who merely visit the presence of God often do so with urgency but not consistency. They come when they need clarity, comfort, or breakthrough—but they leave before intimacy is formed. Visiting may bring inspiration, but dwelling births revelation. Dwelling is where God speaks in whispers, where mysteries unfold slowly, and where the soul learns to recognize His voice in stillness.

Scripture affirms this rhythm. Psalm 91 begins, "He who dwells in the secret place of the Most High shall abide under the shadow of the Almighty" (NKJV). Dwelling leads to abiding, and abiding leads to revelation, protection, and power. Jesus echoed this in John 15:4: "Abide in Me, and I in you" (NKJV). The disciples didn't just visit Jesus; they walked with Him, they ate with Him, they listened, questioned, and lingered. And because they dwelled, they received revelation that changed the world. In that dwelling, we find the courage to live boldly from knowing.

A Launchpad for Boldness

Quiet beginnings are sacred catalysts. *Living Out Loud* by Iyanla Vanzant challenges readers to stop hiding and start showing up as their authentic selves. She affirms that living out loud means embracing truth, shedding shame, and walking boldly in purpose, echoing the transformation from whisper to legacy.

Whispers are often overlooked, but they carry the seed of transformation. A whisper from God—a nudge, a conviction, a gentle prompting—has become the foundation for my testimony. It's the still small voice that called me to speak, to write, to lead, and to take risks.

God rarely begins with a shout. He often starts with a whisper, like a gentle prompting or a subtle shift in your spirit. This is what I experienced. God's prompting led me into ministry and a teaching career after twenty-eight years in a hospital bedside setting. For nearly three decades, I stood at the threshold of life and death, holding hands, offering comfort, and witnessing the sacred vulnerability of humanity. I thought that was my lifelong assignment—and in many ways, it was.

But purpose has layers, and God often unfolds them gradually. His whisper came to me as a nudge that wouldn't go away. At first, I resisted. The idea of stepping away from the familiar rhythm of hospital corridors into the unknown world of teaching felt daunting. I questioned the timing and whether I was truly hearing God. But the whisper persisted. It spoke through Scripture, through conversations, through moments of stillness. And eventually, I realized that the same compassion I had poured out at the bedside was now being redirected to nurture souls, to teach truth, and to shepherd hearts in a different kind of healing space.

The addition of ministry eight years into my nursing career wasn't just a career shift; it was a covenant shift. It required me to trust that God would give me the strength and wisdom to balance it all. The years I spent in healthcare weren't wasted because they prepared me for something bigger. And now, as I teach, minister, and mentor, I carry those years with me as sacred training. All along, God was calling me deeper. And I've learned that when purpose evolves, obedience must follow.

Before we can live loudly, we must listen deeply. Whispers require discernment. You become bold when you hear the whisper, and God whispers because He's close. His voice doesn't need to thunder when His presence is near. Whispers are reserved for relationships, for those who choose proximity over performance. They require attention, intention, and a heart tuned to hear. In a world that demands loud answers and instant clarity, God invites us into quiet trust. He speaks softly so we'll draw nearer, not just to hear but to know. And often, that whisper marks the beginning of something holy.

> **Before we can live loudly, we must listen deeply.**

Zechariah 4:10 reminds us, "Do not despise these small beginnings, for the Lord rejoices to see the work begin" (NLT). Every great move of God has started with a whisper, a nudge, a stirring, or a quiet prompting in the soul. Your whisper moment matters. It may feel small or uncertain, but it carries the weight of divine intention. The whisper is the seed, and when nurtured with obedience and faith, it grows into legacy.

Legacy is built through daily obedience. Every time you say yes to God, you're planting seeds that will outlive you.

> *Your whisper moment matters.*

Living loudly from a whisper means declaring, "This is real. I will build here. I will believe here. I will move from here."

Living loudly from a whisper requires courage. It means saying yes when the details are incomplete, trusting that clarity will follow commitment. It means speaking truth before the crowd

> *Legacy is built through daily obedience.*

affirms it, anchoring your voice in conviction rather than consensus. It's mentoring others while your own questions remain unanswered, or counseling others while you are still hurting, because legacy is built on presence. Your yes can inspire others to believe.

To mentor is to listen for the whispers others may not yet trust. You activate those whispers when you affirm the nudge, when you say, "I see it too." You

> *Clarity will follow commitment.*

don't instruct from ego; you inquire from empathy. You ask the kinds of questions that make space for sacred stirrings.

Sometimes, you carry whispers that are still forming. In your own obedience, you are both living loudly and helping others do the same. Your faith can create ripple effects that outlive your lifetime. And your story, especially the parts you're still walking through, can become someone else's roadmap. The whisper is not just for you; it's for those who will follow your echo.

Writing is one of the most powerful ways to live loudly from a whisper. This is the reason this book exists. A single page can resound across generations. By writing this book, I took what God whispered and shaped it into a life of legacy. A private devotion from these pages can become someone's pivot point. The reflection guide can become spiritual scaffolding. One chapter in this book can become someone's surrender. You don't have to be loud to be heard; you only need to be faithful, and faithfulness is the loudest sermon obedience can ever preach.

> *The whisper is not just for you; it's for those who will follow your echo.*

> *You don't have to be loud to be heard; you only need to be faithful.*

Biblical Examples of Legacy

Legacy in the kingdom of God is never about fame; it's about faithfulness. Abraham's legacy began with a quiet call and a bold response. His faith didn't just shape his own story; it birthed nations and became the blueprint for belief. Mary's legacy was

> *Legacy in the kingdom of God is never about fame; it's about faithfulness.*

sealed in a single word: yes. Because of her obedience, the Savior entered the world. Paul's legacy was forged in letters written from prison cells and on missionary journeys. His words still shape the Church, reminding us that legacy is not confined by circumstance.

Each of these lives began with a whisper, a divine invitation to trust and obey. Each whisper became a ripple that echoed through generations. Your legacy may begin in quiet places, but when rooted in obedience, it carries eternal weight. Legacy is not just what we leave behind; it's what we live now, in faith, surrender, and purpose.

The point of a legacy isn't to leave your own mark but to mark God's goodness in as many stories as possible. Legacy rarely begins with a spotlight. More often, it's born through whispers that stir the soul and call for obedience. Scripture offers us tender portraits of those who responded to soft invitations and, in doing so, shaped history. Ananias, tucked away in Acts 9, received a quiet instruction: Go find Saul. No fanfare, no public commission, just a whisper. Yet that whisper became the hinge on which Paul's ministry turned, launching a legacy that would echo through generations.

Philip was told simply to go toward Gaza. And in that obedience, he encountered the Ethiopian official whose conversion carried the Gospel into new lands. Barnabas, known as the son of encouragement, didn't preach a sermon or write a letter; he whispered affirmation. His encouragement transformed John Mark from a ministry dropout into a Gospel author. One gentle nudge and a legacy was reborn.

These stories remind us that legacy does not require loud beginnings. It requires faithful stewardship of soft invitations. The whisper is enough when it's God's.

In educational spaces, whispers are often ignored in favor of rubrics and metrics. But true teaching incorporates spirit. When you guide students, the whisper may be embedded in how you affirm their instincts or challenge their assumptions. The whisper shows up when conversation detours into spiritual wisdom and when a moment of frustration becomes a lesson in grace. I don't just teach or preach content; I teach calling. You model what it means to hear God during work hours. You help people live loudly by responding to what was whispered into their journey.

Public Testimony

Public testimony is the practice that amplifies the whisper. It's the moment you choose to share what God has done, even if your voice trembles. Whether through writing, speaking, mentoring, or simply naming your story aloud, testimony turns private revelation into communal light. You don't always have to get it right, so long as you show up. When you testify, you give others permission to believe, hope, and follow. I can testify that God has used my brokenness, disappointments, pains, and betrayals to create a beautiful mosaic for others to see and from which they can learn to trust God even when all is shattered.

When you live from a whisper, your life becomes a message, and that message multiplies through influence, mentorship, and storytelling. I did not

> *When you live from a whisper, your life becomes a message.*

know the assignment had already found me. I was waiting for clarity, I was waiting to feel good, I was waiting for the tears to stop—but God had already whispered through the quiet moments of counseling others who were also hurting. In the midst of my own ache, I was unknowingly walking in purpose. That whisper wasn't loud, but it was persistent. It came through shared pain, through sacred conversations, and through the healing I offered while still bleeding myself. That was my call to obedience: when I chose to serve while still broken.

My tears carried the weight of betrayal, of being overlooked, of feeling discarded by spaces I had poured my life into. I grieved not just the loss of a role but the loss of relationships I thought were rooted in loyalty. Yet in that grief, God was gathering every tear and storing them as testimony (Psalm 56:8). What felt like abandonment became the soil for deeper compassion. What felt like rejection became the doorway to revelation. Far from wasted, my tears were woven into the very fabric of my calling.

Now I see how obedience responds to divine invitation, with or without emotional resolution. God didn't ask me to be ready; He asked me to be willing. And in saying yes, even through tears, I stepped into an assignment that was birthed from surrender. The assignment didn't come after healing; it came through it. And every tear I cried became a seed of empathy, a wellspring of wisdom, and a quiet confirmation that purpose often finds us in the fog.

Mentorship and discipleship are opportunities to pour into others what God has faithfully poured into you. Even if you don't have all the answers, you need only offer your journey as a living well of wisdom and faith. In doing so, you create a legacy that outlasts seasons and circumstances.

Your story holds power. When you share it with honesty and hope, you become a lighthouse, shining your light through the fog. Your life can guide others safely to shore.

This book is part of my legacy, and it started as a whisper. Here's how you can steward your own whisper:

1. **Document it.** I journaled the whisper I heard, even when I was unsure what it even was.
2. **Declare it softly first.** I spoke it to myself several times a week, before it became a full mission.
3. **Discern before you shout.** Not every whisper is ready to be broadcasted. Some need shaping, and some need growth. So I kept mine quiet until now.
4. **Act before you're ready.** Don't wait for public proof. I began with private obedience and wrote as I heard the whisper.

Amplifying the Whisper Without Losing the Intimacy

As the whisper became work—ministry, career, leadership, and purpose—there was a risk of diluting the message. I had to fight to preserve the sacredness of the original call. As you amplify your whisper, ask:

- Does this still feel connected to the initial nudge?
- Am I living from faith or merely functioning from habit?
- Have I paused to recalibrate intimacy in the midst of amplification?

To amplify the whisper requires naming the quiet truths stirring within you. Perhaps it's a message you've carried for years, a story you've hesitated to share, or a calling you've only admitted in prayer. What would it look like to give that whisper volume? What would it look like to let that whisper rise into boldness, not for attention, but for impact? This is your light, and the world needs it. Amplifying the whisper in your life means tuning in to God's subtle nudges and responding with intentionality. Instead of trying to make the whisper louder, focus on making your life quieter, more focused, and more surrendered so you can hear it clearly.

Here are some powerful ways you can amplify that whisper:

1. Create Sacred Stillness

Example: A busy mom begins waking up thirty minutes earlier to sit in silence before her day begins. Over time, she starts sensing God's direction in areas she'd been praying about for years.

2. Respond Before You Feel Ready

Whispers often come before confidence. Obedience amplifies clarity. Movement activates momentum.

Example: A young man feels a tug to mentor teens but doubts his qualifications. He says yes anyway. That simple obedience opens doors to deeper purpose and unexpected impact.

3. Surround Yourself with Spirit-Led Voices

Community helps you discern. Wise counsel confirms God's voice (Proverbs 11:14). Isolation muffles the whisper, while connection amplifies it.

Example: A woman joins a small group where people speak life and truth. Their encouragement helps her recognize the whisper she'd been ignoring: that she's called to write and teach.

4. Journal the Nudges

Writing helps you track divine patterns. Journaling turns whispers into roadmaps.

Example: A college student starts writing down every moment that feels like a divine nudge. Over time, patterns emerge, revealing a calling toward advocacy.

5. Fast from Noise

Noise competes with God's whisper. While normally about food, you can also fast from noise to gain focus. Less distraction equals more revelation.

Example: A pastor takes a week off from social media and entertainment. In the quiet, he hears God speak about a new direction for his ministry.

Remember: The whisper is already speaking. Are you close enough to hear it?

Finishing Well

Legacy isn't just about how you start; it's about how you finish. Staying faithful to the end is one of the greatest testimonies you can leave. Staying the course requires that you guard your

> *Legacy isn't just about how you start; it's about how you finish.*

heart, stay rooted in God's Word, and remain humble and teachable. What trail do you want to leave? What do you want people to remember about your life? What values, truths, and love will you pass on?

Living loudly from a whisper means

- building what no one sees—because you heard what no one heard.
- speaking when it's unpopular—because the nudge is too holy to ignore.
- praying when prayer seems unanswered—because the goal is intimacy.

May 2 Timothy 4:7 be your testimony: "I have fought the good fight, I have finished the race, I have kept the faith" (NIV).

Reflection and Application

Illustration: A whisper can birth a legacy. One unseen act of obedience can ripple through lives you'll never meet.

Scripture Focus: *"What I tell you in the dark, speak in the daylight; what is whispered in your ear, proclaim from the roofs."* (Matthew 10:27, NIV)

Devotional Thought: Whispers from God are not meant to stay secret. The nudge, the prompting, the idea that came in solitude is preparation for public proclamation. Your current influence may look loud, but it was birthed in stillness. Let your life continue to echo what heaven once whispered.

Questions for Reflection:

- How can you live more intentionally today to build the legacy you want to leave?
- Who in your life can you pour into or encourage?
- What whisper from God still guides your loudest impact?
- What whisper are you ready to amplify?

Action Steps:

- Write a "legacy letter" to your future self or loved ones, describing the life you want to live.
- Share your story with someone who needs hope.
- Revisit journal entries about past nudges that felt minor at the time. Identify one that blossomed into visible impact. Share it in writing, testimony, or tribute to encourage another.

Prayer:

"Lord, help me never forget the whisper that started it all. May my voice never outpace my intimacy with You. Father, let my obedience to Your whisper create a legacy that honors You. May my life echo Your purpose. Amen."

CLOSING

Let the Whisper Echo

You don't need a platform to make an impact. You don't need a spotlight to leave a legacy. All you need is a whisper and the courage to obey it. When you live from a whisper, your life will echo in ways you may never fully see. And that echo will carry the sound of faith, hope, and purpose for generations to come.

So, keep living from the whisper. Let it roar in legacy. Let it amplify in love. Let it rise in all your encounters.

Closing Blessing

May you walk with sacred slowness, carry peace between life's chapters, and let every whisper shape your next yes.

Additional Resources

Books:

- *He Speaks in the Silence* by Diane Comer
- *The Listening Path: The Creative Art of Attention* by Julia Cameron
- *Anonymous: Jesus' Hidden Years...and Yours* by Alicia Britt Chole
- *God's Voice Within: The Ignatian Way to Discover God's Will* by Mark E. Thibodeaux, SJ
- *Discerning the Voice of God: How to Recognize When God is Speaking* by Priscilla Shirer
- *The Way of Discernment: Spiritual Practices for Decision Making* by Elizabeth Liebert
- *Still Waiting: Hope for When God Doesn't Give You What You Want* by Ann Swindell
- *Sacred Waiting: Waiting on God in a World That Waits for Nothing* by David Timms
- *When God Says Wait* by Elizabeth Laing Thompson
- *Puzzle Pieces of Purpose* by Sigourney Rosario
- *Pursuing Purpose: 5 Keys to Fulfilling Your God-Given Purpose* by Kyra Lanae

- *Pieces to Purpose: Unbreakable Women Who Refused to Give Up* by Alicia Raffkind (and contributors)
- *Permission Granted: Be Who You Were Made to Be and Let Go of the Rest* by Melissa Camara Wilkins
- *Celebration of Discipline: The Path to Spiritual Growth* by Richard J. Foster
- *Letting Go: The Pathway of Surrender* by David R. Hawkins
- *The Gift of the Unexpected: Discovering Who You Were Meant to Be When Life Goes Off Plan* by Jillian Benfield
- *Faith in the Fog: Believing in What You Cannot See* by Jeff Lucas
- *Faith in the Fog of War: Let Us Die to Make Men Free* by Chris Plekenpol
- *Whisper Loudly: Listening to God with My Whole Heart* by Polly Rhea Harper
- *The Whisper Within: Navigating Life with Your Inner Voice* by Khalid A. Haaziq
- *Lectio Divina: The Medieval Experience of Reading* by Duncan Robertson

Articles:

- Patheos – "Is It God or Me? 7 Ways to Discern God's Nudges" (https://www.patheos.com/blogs/fabricoffaith/2024/03/is-it-god-or-me-7-ways-to-discern-gods-nudges/)
- The Biblical Truth – "Understanding God's Nudges" (https://thebiblicaltruth.com/the-divine-whisper-understanding-gods-nudges-in-scripture/)

Additional Resources

- Faith in the Divine – "Divine Whispers: When God Talks to Me in My Head" (https://faithinthedivine.com/god-talks-to-me-in-my-head/)
- Desiring God – "Already, Not Yet" (https://www.desiringgod.org/articles/already-not-yet)

About the Author

Dr. Felicia "Fefe" Bessman is a woman of grace and purpose, passionately serving others through every facet of her life. She is an Assistant Professor and a dedicated Family Nurse Practitioner, blending academic excellence with compassionate care. As a pastor's wife, counselor, and mentor, Felicia walks alongside others with wisdom and empathy, offering guidance rooted in faith.

Her heart for missions has taken her across borders as a medical missionary to Central America and Africa, where she brings healing and hope to underserved communities. Whether in the classroom, clinic, or church, Felicia lives to empower others to discover and walk boldly in their God-given purpose.

Made in the USA
Coppell, TX
20 January 2026

67026986R00100